The Tofu Cookbook

By the same author:

Easy Vegan Cooking

The Tofu Cookbook

Leah Leneman

Thorsons

Thorsons
An Imprint of HarperCollins*Publishers*
77–85 Fulham Palace Road,
Hammersmith, London W6 8JB

Published by Thorsons 1992, 1998
7 9 10 8

Illustrations by Daisy Kelly

Many of these recipes previously appeared in
The International Tofu Cookery Book and *Soya Foods Cookery*

A catalogue record for this book is
available from the British Library

ISBN 0 7225 3667 4

Typeset by Harper Phototypesetters Limited,
Northampton, England
Printed and bound in Great Britain by
Martins the Printers Limited, Berwick upon Tweed

Contents

Introduction

Tofu – also known as soya (soy) bean curd – has been a staple food of the Orient for centuries. In recent years it has been growing in popularity in the West to a phenomenal extent. There are several reasons for this.

The first is its nutritional advantages. The modern Western diet, which is high in saturated animal fats and cholesterol, is strongly implicated in obesity and heart disease so many people are seeking alternatives. Tofu is high in protein yet low in calories and free of cholesterol. Puréed, it can provide a rich, creamy-tasting substitute for mayonnaise, soured cream, whipped cream and other dairy products, with a fraction of the calories. Mashed, it can be used in place of eggs with none of the cholesterol content. And, deep-fried or sautéed, it can provide the same service for dishes normally containing meat, fish or chicken.

Anyone tasting plain tofu for the first time is surprised at how bland it is, but it is this blandness which is one of its greatest assets since it can absorb any kind of flavouring. And, unlike soya (soy) beans themselves, tofu is very easy to digest, and can be eaten even by young children or the elderly with no harmful consequences. It is also low in cost.

Another reason more and more people are trying tofu is compassion. The public is gradually becoming aware of the full horrors of factory farming, and slowly realizing that even a lacto-vegetarian diet, which avoids slaughterhouse products, does not go far enough. The enforced continued lactation of cows, the separation of calf from cow (the former often going to the veal pen, the latter to produce milk for human consumption), and the battery cage are all part of the system. Cutting down on, or giving up, dairy produce is made much easier with the use of soya (soy) milk and tofu, and all the recipes in this book are dairy-free.

Not only animals, but human beings all over the globe would benefit from the change, for at present a large proportion of the world's soya (soy) bean crop is fed to animals, an extremely inefficient use of global resources. Indeed, if the protein available from the soya (soy) bean crop grown today – let alone the additional amount which could be grown if more land were released from grazing livestock – were utilized directly by human beings, a large percentage of the world's protein deficiency could be wiped out tomorrow. It should be emphasized that, unlike TVP-type meat substitutes, which require a fairly sophisticated technology, tofu is simple enough to be made in any home.

Of course, tofu sales would not be growing by such leaps and bounds were altruism the sole motive. People may care about their health, about animals, or about the world food problem, but few of them would care enough to go on buying ever-increasing amounts of tofu unless they actually *liked* it. Tofu is fun – it can be used in more interesting and varied ways than any other single food. The cook who is tired of tofu must be tired of life.

Types of Tofu

There are basically three types of tofu: silken tofu is very soft; medium tofu is firmer (you could lift it but would need to be careful as it is still delicate and a piece could break off); firm tofu can be held up as a block without breaking. In the USA any health-food store or supermarket that stocks tofu will normally offer all three types; this is not yet the case in Britain.

SOFT OR 'SILKEN' TOFU

Silken tofu is a Japanese product made in a different way from other types of tofu (the curds and whey are not separated). In Britain the only available form of this is a long-life product made by Morinaga. It is useful because it keeps for months (without refrigeration), and it is a pure, high-quality product, but it has a more distinctive flavour than most tofu, which may not please all palates. At delicatessens and Oriental shops it is sometimes possible to find boxes of do-it-yourself 'House' tofu, containing soya (soy) milk powder and a coagulant. This makes a large quantity of very soft tofu (but see below).

MEDIUM TOFU

If you make your own tofu using Epsom salts or lemon juice then you are likely to produce medium tofu (particularly if you do not press it for too long). If you buy fresh tofu at a wholefood shop it may also be medium tofu. However, most commercially produced tofu in Britain is vacuum-packed and firm rather than medium. Medium tofu is therefore the least readily available in the UK, though it is easily found in the USA. There is now a Morinaga 'firm' silken tofu available in some health-food stores which is actually medium in texture. Medium tofu is found in

Chinese supermarkets in many large towns and cities in Britain. However, Chinese tofu has a strong flavour which makes it unsuitable for many recipes, particularly desserts, though naturally it is fine for Oriental dishes. Another way of getting medium tofu is to follow the instructions on a packet of Japanese 'House' tofu but use only ⅔ pint (340ml, 1½ cups) water. Immediately after adding the coagulant and stirring the mixture, pour it into a container, cover it and leave until cool. Then slide a knife round the sides, fill the container with water, cover again and refrigerate until needed. In texture it will be similar to Chinese tofu (though unlike Chinese tofu it is not very satisfactory for deep-frying), but the taste is totally different, being quite sweet. Because of its taste and texture I have found converted Japanese tofu ideal for recipes – both savoury and sweet – which would normally call for a milk custard. One packet prepared in this way will yield approximately ¾ lb (340g, 1½ cups) tofu.

FIRM TOFU

This is the kind found vacuum-packed in shops throughout Britain. If it is the only kind available and is used in a recipe calling for soft or medium tofu to be puréed, then extra liquid should be added to make it as smooth as possible.

More Unusual Forms of Tofu

SMOKED TOFU

An enterprising individual in Britain discovered that smoking tofu gave it a new texture and delicious taste, and it has proved very popular indeed. It can be used 'raw' straight from the packet, sliced in sandwiches or diced in salads. Thinly sliced and grilled (broiled) or fried it becomes crispy.

MARINATED TOFU

One of the most popular ways of preparing tofu is to marinate it in a mixture of soy sauce and ginger, so someone decided to package tofu prepared in this way; this product too has become very popular in Britain, though I do not think it can be found in America. Its most obvious use is in a Chinese stir-fry, but I have found that after freezing it is delicious deep-fried.

FERMENTED TOFU

This can be found in jars and tins at Chinese supermarkets. Fermented tofu is said to be a little like Camembert cheese, but the salt concentration is much too high for it to be palatable on its own. It does, however, add a pleasant, distinctive flavour to a tofu dip. Put a packet of Morinaga silken tofu into a liquidizer with 2 tbs vegetable oil, 2–3 cubes fermented tofu, and 2 tsp lemon juice, and blend ingredients thoroughly.

FROZEN TOFU

Ordinary tofu can be frozen; when thawed it will have a 'meatier' consistency than when fresh. It is a good idea to slice the tofu before freezing it. It can be thawed by simply putting it in the refrigerator or leaving it out for a few hours, but the preferred way is to pour boiling water over it and leave for about 10 minutes. Drain the slices and then – very gently to avoid breaking them – squeeze them. This is an essential step as otherwise they will make a dish watery. Dried-frozen tofu, which is very convenient as it can be kept in the larder for emergency use at any time, is available at some wholefood shops.

DEEP-FRIED TOFU

Some Chinese shops sell tofu that has already been deep-fried, though this tends to be sold in rather large quantities. If done properly – i.e. at the right temperature – deep-frying is not at all unhealthy, as very little oil is absorbed by the tofu. To deep fry tofu, either invest in a cooking thermometer and heat the oil to 350°F (180°C) before lowering the tofu cubes into the oil or, better still, use a deep-fat fryer, which automatically regulates the temperature.

Other Soya (Soy) Foods

SOYA (SOY) MILK

It is now very easy to buy this milk in Britain and the USA. In Britain there are cartons sweetened with raw sugar, with honey or with apple juice, and cartons of unsweetened milk, some made from organic soya (soy) beans. Plamil, the pioneers of British soya milk, fortify theirs with vitamin B_{12}. America gets really tasty soymilks from Japan. There are also cartons flavoured with carob, chocolate, banana, strawberry and coconut. Thanks to the wide variety of soya (soy) milks available, if you try one kind and don't like it there are plenty of others to choose from until you find one you like.

SOYA (SOY) YOGURT

It is now quite easy to obtain flavoured soya (soy) yogurts in Britain (though not in the USA). They are very tasty, but do remember that many of them are long-life and therefore do not have the beneficial effects on the digestive system that a 'live' yogurt has. At the time of writing there is one plain (natural) soya (soy) yogurt (imported into Britain from France under the Soyasun brand name).

Whatever one thinks of the health claims for yogurt, there is no denying that it is marvellous for the digestion and is particularly valuable in a high-fibre diet as it aids the digestion of such foods. The name of the commonest form of yogurt culture, *Lactobacillus bulgaricus*, may mislead some people into thinking there is a dairy derivative in it, but such is not the case. It is, however, necessary to check carefully the ingredients of the ferment you buy as some do have dairy derivatives added to them.

It is very easy to make soya (soy) yogurt at home, and a wide-rimmed vacuum flask is as effective as a yogurt-maker for the purpose. It can be made from any of the soya (soy) milks on the market, even the unsweetened ones. Just heat the milk to a lukewarm temperature (if it is too hot then cool it down to lukewarm) and follow the instructions on the packet of ferment. The first batch or two of soya (soy) yogurt is never very flavourful, but if you keep using a spoonful of soya (soy) yogurt to make the next batch, it gets better and better, and it will keep going for many months before a new packet of ferment is required. You can freeze a little yogurt when it is at its best or if you are going away on holiday and then defrost it and use it as a starter for a new batch when required.

SOYA (SOY) MAYONNAISE
Mayonnaise-type dressings made from tofu are now readily available in health-food stores. Tofu mayonnaise is easy to prepare; for an example see the recipe for Potato salad on p 27

BEAN CURD STICKS OR SHEETS
These can be found in Chinese supermarkets and are used in Chinese cooking to produce delicacies such as 'mock duck'. In spite of their name they are not actually tofu at all; they are made from the skin which is skimmed off in the making of soya (soy) milk.

TEMPEH
Pronounced 'tempay' (with the accent on the first syllable), this food originated in Indonesia. Soya (soy) beans are bound together by spores which cause them to ferment and join into a solid mass. Tempeh is high in protein, low in fat, and cholesterol free. Unlike tofu, it has a high fibre content, and because of the fermentation process the fibre is easily digested. Tempeh is found in frozen-food compartments of some wholefood shops.

SOY SAUCE
The purest forms of this well-known Chinese seasoning are shoyu and tamari (the only difference is that tamari has wheat added). Soy sauces available at supermarkets are often inferior products with additives, so unless buying a product labelled shoyu or tamari check the ingredients carefully.

OTHER SOYA (SOY) FOODS

MISO

Miso is a high-protein fermented soya (soy) food used as a flavouring. It is a concentrated paste so, although it is expensive to buy, very little is needed for any one dish and therefore it represents good value for money. Ideally miso should be added to dishes at the last possible moment, or eaten uncooked, because boiling destroys the valuable digestion-aiding enzymes. After opening, miso should be kept refrigerated and airtight and will then last for months (if not years). There are several different types of miso available, the differences being in saltiness and flavour; any one of them can be used in a recipe calling for miso.

SOYA (SOY) CHEESE

As the biggest stumbling block for most people in giving up dairy products is cheese, it is not surprising that much effort is going into developing soya (soy)-based cheeses. Most of the American so-called soy cheeses contain casein, a dairy derivative, though there is one brand, Soymage, which does not. At the time of writing, a British firm is manufacturing an ever-increasing range of soya-based hard cheeses under the brand name Scheese. All of these products can be used in any dish calling for hard cheese, though none is particularly palatable uncooked. Plamil was the first company in Britain to produce a soft soya-based cheese, called Veeze, which is a sandwich spread rather like processed cheese but which can also be incorporated into cooked dishes. An easy way of making a soft cheese is to pour homemade soya (soy) yogurt into a large square of muslin and tie it up to drip for several hours. Quite a large quantity of yogurt is needed to make rather a small quantity of cheese, but it really tastes delicious and can be flavoured in a number of different ways (e.g. with chives for a savoury spread or pineapple for a sweet spread).

Notes on the Recipes

The addition of the word 'style' to every type of cuisine featured in this book is quite deliberate, and I make no pretence that the recipes are necessarily authentic. They were adapted by me using ingredients which were obtainable and which I liked.

All the recipes in this book are intended to serve four people for lunch or dinner (with perhaps a sweet to follow). However, this can only be a general guideline as appetites vary so much, and if you serve soup or side dishes then the recipes might feed more.

Many cookery books state that you must not mix Imperial and metric measurements since they are not exactly the same and could unbalance a recipe. However, the recipes in this book are sufficiently robust to allow you to be flexible and mix Imperial, metric and American measurements as you please.

As the recipes show, I tend to use canned beans rather than cooking them myself. Obviously using dried beans is very much cheaper, and canned beans have to be rinsed very thoroughly to get rid of the excess salt (and often sugar as well), but since I work full time and am busy at weekends as well, I find the convenience of using canned beans outweighs the other factors. If you prefer to use dried beans, as a rough guide 4–5 oz (115–140g) dried beans is equivalent to a 14–16 oz (400g) tin of beans.

Finally, a word about one ingredient likely to be unfamiliar to American readers and another unfamiliar to many British readers: yeast extract and nutritional yeast. Yeast extract is a thick, salty paste with a vaguely 'meaty' flavour; in the USA it is most likely to be found in health-food stores under its Australian brand name of Vegemite. Nutritional yeast comes in powder or flake form and has a vaguely 'cheesy' taste. Americans could order it from The Good-Tasting Food Co., PO Box 188, Summertown, TN 38483. Britons will find it in health-food stores as Marigold Engevita nutritional yeast flakes.

Making Tofu at Home

The method below does not necessarily make the smoothest tofu, nor the greatest quantity. It does, however, make a delicious firm tofu, and it is so much quicker and easier than any other method I have read about that I can't imagine making it any other way.

There are various coagulants which can be used to curdle the soya (soy) milk, the commonest being lemon juice, Epsom salts, and a seawater product called nigari. All of these are suitable, but the most strongly recommended is nigari, for three reasons: (1) it makes the firmest tofu, (2) it makes the best-tasting tofu, and (3) it is virtually foolproof. Nigari has become readily available at wholefood shops, but anyone unable to get hold of it in Britain can order it by post from Real Foods, 37 Broughton Street, Edinburgh EH1 3JU.

In order to make tofu the following are required:

a large saucepan (holding at least 6 pints [3½ litres, 15 cups])
a liquidizer
a colander
a small box (about 6in × 4in [15cm × 10cm]) with small holes punched in the bottom and sides (the holes can be punched into an ordinary plastic sandwich box, and the sides cut off the lid so it fits in on top)
a large piece of muslin (about 2 ft [0.75m])
a small piece of muslin to fit inside the box

If you are making tofu to be mashed or puréed rather than sliced or cubed, you can omit the box and just use a colander lined with muslin.

1   The night before, cover $^1/_2$ lb (225g, 1 cup) soya (soy) beans with boiling water and leave them to soak. In the morning drain and rinse. Place a cupful of the soaked beans in a liquidizer, add a cupful of cold water and blend. Then add about 2 cupfuls of boiling water to the liquidizer and blend again. If your liquidizer is not large enough then a smaller quantity can be done each time as long as the proportions are kept more or less the same – it is not necessary to measure with any great precision when making tofu.

2   Place the large piece of muslin over the saucepan and carefully pour the contents of the liquidizer into it. Pull up the sides to make it into a sack so that the soya (soy) milk runs through, and squeeze gently to get all of the liquid into the saucepan. (The pulp left in the muslin is called okara and can be used in savouries; it is high in protein but, unlike tofu, is not very easy to digest.)

3   Once all of the beans have been used up put the saucepan on to a medium to high heat and bring to the boil, stirring the bottom from time to time. Keep a careful eye on it because it can boil over very suddenly and dramatically. As soon as it reaches boiling point, turn the heat down very low so it is still simmering but no longer threatening to erupt. Leave it to simmer for about 3 minutes.

4   Meanwhile, put 1 heaped tsp nigari or other coagulant into a teacup. Fill it half full of boiling water and stir well. Remove the soya (soy) milk from the heat, then gently stir in the dissolved coagulant, trying to make certain it has been stirred through all of the liquid. Leave for about 3 minutes, by which time curds should have formed.

5   Place the muslin-lined box (if used) in the colander, then gradually pour the contents of the saucepan into it, so that the whey runs through and the curds settle in the box. Then put the colander over the empty saucepan to continue to drain, and place a heavy object (about 2 lb [900g]) on top. Leave for an hour or so before unmoulding. Half a pound (225g, 1 cup) soya (soy) beans will make about $^3/_4$ lb (340g, $1^1/_2$ cups) tofu (though it can vary by 2 oz [55g, $^1/_4$ cup] either way).

If the tofu is not to be used immediately it should be stored in the refrigerator in an airtight container of water, where it will keep for about a week. (Most instructions tell you to change the water every day, but if the container is left undisturbed then this really is not necessary.)

If the tofu has been stored and is to be sautéed or deep-fried rather than mashed or puréed it is best to drain it thoroughly first and then wrap it in a tea towel (dish towel) for a short while to get rid of surplus water. Deep-fried tofu will keep for several days longer in the fridge; store the cubes dry, in a polythene bag.

SOYA (SOY) FLOUR TOFU

Whisk 1 part soya (soy) flour into 3 parts boiling water. Simmer for 15–20 minutes, stirring occasionally. Add approximately 1 tsp coagulant per 2 pints (1.1 l, 5 cups) liquid and proceed as above. Do not expect the result to be the same as when using beans. The curd will be much smaller, and no matter how long you press it, soya (soy) flour tofu never becomes firm enough to sauté or deep-fry. It can, however, be used in recipes requiring mashed or puréed tofu.

1
Soups
& Dips

Cream of lentil soup

No additional fat is used for this soup, making it ideal for slimmers and others watching their fat intake. The combination of tofu and lentils makes it a high-protein dish.

IMPERIAL/METRIC		AMERICAN
1	onion	1
4 oz (115g)	red lentils	$^3/_4$ cup
2$^1/_2$ pints (1.4 l)	water	6$^1/_3$ cups
2	bay leaves	2
2–3 tsp	yeast extract	2–3 tsp
8–10 oz (225–285g)	soft or medium tofu	1–1$^1/_4$ cups
as required	sea salt	as required
as required	freshly ground black pepper	as required
as required	chopped parsley	as required

1   Chop the onion. Put the onion and cleaned lentils in a saucepan and cover with the water. Add the bay leaves and yeast extract and bring to the boil. Lower the heat, cover the pan, and simmer for about 15 minutes, by which time the lentils should be tender.

2   Cool the mixture slightly. Remove the bay leaves and pour the mixture into a liquidizer. Add the tofu and blend until smooth.

3   Return the blended mixture to the saucepan and heat gently. Season to taste, and serve sprinkled with a little parsley.

Cream of cauliflower and potato soup

Combining tofu with potato and cauliflower gives a rich creaminess, more usually associated with an undesirably high fat content.

IMPERIAL/METRIC		AMERICAN
1 small	cauliflower	1 small
1	onion	1
1 lb (455g)	potatoes	1 lb
1¹/₂ pints (850ml)	vegetable stock or water	3³/₄ cups
¹/₂ lb (225g)	soft or medium tofu	1 cup
as required	sea salt	as required
as required	freshly ground black pepper	as required
1 tbs	vegetable margarine	1 tbs
as required	chopped parsley	as required

1   Chop the cauliflower, onion and potatoes into dice, cover and cook in the stock or water until very soft. Cool briefly, then pour into a liquidizer, add the tofu, and blend thoroughly.
2   Return the mixture to the saucepan, add seasoning and the margarine, and reheat gently. Serve topped with chopped parsley.

Cream of celery soup

This creamy soup is not only low in fat but low in calories as well. Serve it to weightwatchers – and anyone else who enjoys a good soup.

IMPERIAL/METRIC		AMERICAN
1 head	celery	1 head
1	onion	1
2 tbs	vegetable oil	2 tbs
1³/₄ pints (990ml)	water or vegetable stock	4 cups
as required	sea salt	as required
as required	freshly ground black pepper	as required
1 tsp	dried mixed herbs	1 tsp
¹/₂ lb (225g)	soft or medium tofu	1 cup
2 tbs	chopped parsley	2 tbs

1   Scrub and chop the celery. Chop the onion. Sauté both in the oil for a few minutes.
2   Add the water or stock, seasoning and herbs. Bring to the boil, then lower the heat, cover, and simmer for about 20 minutes.
3   Pour into a liquidizer and leave to cool slightly. Add the tofu and blend thoroughly.
4   Pour back into the saucepan and reheat gently. Serve topped with parsley.

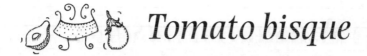 # Tomato bisque

A bisque is a creamy soup that retains the texture of the main ingredient.

IMPERIAL/METRIC		AMERICAN
2	onions	2
2 tins	tomatoes	2 cans
(about 14oz		(14–16 oz each)
[400g] each)		
²/₃ pint (340ml)	water	1¹/₂ cups
¹/₂ lb (225g)	soft or medium tofu	1 cup
1 tbs	vegetable margarine	1 tbs
	sea salt and freshly ground pepper	

1 Chop the onions finely. Put them into a saucepan with the tomatoes (chop them coarsely with a spoon while adding them – or use canned chopped tomatoes), the water and seasonings. Bring to the boil, then lower the heat and simmer, uncovered, for 20–30 minutes.
2 Put the tofu into a liquidizer with the margarine and a few spoonfuls of liquid from the soup. Blend thoroughly.
3 Add the contents of the liquidizer to the saucepan. Heat gently over a very low heat and serve immediately.

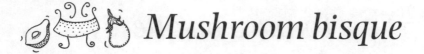 # Mushroom bisque

Tofu adds a creamy base to this soup, leaving the taste and texture of the mushrooms to the fore.

IMPERIAL/METRIC		AMERICAN
2	onions	2
2 tbs	vegetable margarine	2 tbs
³/₄ lb (340g)	mushrooms	6 cups
1 tbs	paprika	1 tbs
¹/₄ tsp	cayenne pepper	¹/₄ tsp
1 pint (570ml)	vegetable stock or water	2¹/₂ cups
as required	sea salt	as required
as required	freshly ground black pepper	as required
¹/₂ lb (225g)	soft or medium tofu	1 cup
1¹/₂ tbs	vegetable oil	1¹/₂ tbs
3 tsp	lemon juice	3 tsp

1   Chop the onions and sauté in the margarine for 4–5 minutes.
2   Chop the mushrooms finely, add to the onions with the paprika and cayenne and stir. Cover the pan and leave to cook for 7–10 minutes.
3   Stir in the stock or water and the salt and pepper, bring to the boil, and simmer for a further 3–4 minutes.
4   Put the tofu, oil and lemon juice in a liquidizer and blend. Stir this mixture into the saucepan, and heat gently, without allowing it to boil. Taste and adjust seasoning if necessary. Serve immediately.

Chilled cream of cucumber soup

Here is a cold, creamy (but very low-fat) soup that is ideal for a hot summer's day.

IMPERIAL/METRIC		AMERICAN
1	cucumber	1
1	onion	1
1 pint (570ml)	vegetable stock or water	2½ cups
1 tbs	soy sauce	1 tbs
½ lb (225g)	soft or medium tofu	1 cup
1 tbs	vegetable oil	1 tbs
as required	sea salt	as required
as required	freshly ground black pepper	as required

1 Peel and dice the cucumber, keeping some back for garnish. Chop the onion.
2 Put the stock or water, soy sauce, cucumber and onion in a saucepan, and bring to the boil. Lower the heat, cover, and simmer for about 15 minutes.
3 Put the tofu, oil and contents of the saucepan into a liquidizer and blend thoroughly.
4 Season to taste, cool, then chill. Garnish with the reserved cucumber before serving.

Vichyssoise

Tofu transforms a classic French recipe, which would make a good starter for a dinner party.

IMPERIAL/METRIC		AMERICAN
4	leeks	4
1	onion	1
2 oz (55g)	vegetable margarine	$^1/_4$ cup
1 lb (455g)	potatoes	1 lb
1 tbs	paprika	1 tbs
1$^3/_4$ pints (990ml)	vegetable stock or water	4 cups
3 tbs	soy sauce	3 tbs
as required	freshly ground black pepper	as required
$^1/_2$ lb (225g)	soft or medium tofu	1 cup
as required	chopped chives or spring onions (scallions)	as required

1 Chop the leeks and onion finely. Sauté in the margarine for 15–20 minutes over a low heat until tender.
2 Peel the potatoes, or leave the skins on if preferred, and dice them. Add them to the saucepan with the stock or water, soy sauce, and black pepper. Bring to the boil, then cover and simmer for about 20 minutes, until the potatoes are soft. Cool slightly.
3 Put the mixture into a liquidizer with the tofu, and blend thoroughly.
4 Chill, and serve sprinkled with chopped chives or spring onions (scallions).

 # Tofu gumbo

Deep-frying tofu makes it light and chewy, adding a terrific texture to some classic soups. Gumbo comes from the American Deep South and uses okra (ladies' fingers), which is now much more readily available in Britain.

IMPERIAL/METRIC		AMERICAN
¹/₂ lb (225g)	medium or firm tofu	1 cup
2 tbs plus additional for deep-frying	vegetable oil	2 tbs plus additional for deep-frying
1	onion	1
1 small	green (bell) pepper	1 small
¹/₂ lb (225g)	okra (ladies' fingers)	¹/₂ lb
1 tin (about 14 oz [400g])	tomatoes	1 can (14–16 oz)
1¹/₂ pints (850ml)	vegetable stock or water	3³/₄ cups
1	bay leaf	1
2–3 tbs	chopped parsley	2–3 tbs
as required	sea salt	as required
as required	freshly ground black pepper	as required

1 Chop the tofu into small dice and deep-fry in the oil until golden brown. Drain well and set aside.

2 Chop the onion and green (bell) pepper. Clean the okra (ladies' fingers), top and tail them, and chop each one into 2–3 pieces. Sauté these ingredients in the 2 tbs oil for 4–5 minutes, stirring occasionally.

3 Add the tomatoes, stock or water, and bay leaf to the okra (ladies' fingers) mixture, bring to the boil, then lower the heat, cover and simmer for 15–20 minutes.

4 Add the fried tofu, parsley and seasoning, cook for a couple of minutes longer, then serve.

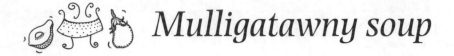

Mulligatawny soup

There are numerous variants on this Anglo-Indian classic, but most of them don't include tofu...

IMPERIAL/METRIC		AMERICAN
1	onion	1
2 sticks	celery	2 sticks
1	carrot	1
1	apple	1
1/2 lb (225g)	tomatoes	1/2 lb
1 oz (30g)	vegetable margarine	2 tbs
1–2 tbs	curry powder	1–2 tbs
2	cloves	2
1 tbs	chopped parsley	1 tbs
1 1/2 pints (850ml)	water	3 3/4 cups
1 tsp	yeast extract	1 tsp
4 oz (115g)	medium or firm tofu	1/2 cup
as required	vegetable oil for deep-frying	as required
1/4 pint (140ml)	soya (soy) milk	2/3 cup
3 tbs	wholewheat flour	3 tbs
as required	sea salt	as required
as required	freshly ground black pepper	as required

1   Chop the onion, celery and carrot finely. Peel and chop the apple; skin the tomatoes and chop them. Sauté all these ingredients in the margarine for about 5 minutes.
2   Stir in the curry powder and cook for a further 1–2 minutes. Add the cloves, parsley, water and yeast extract. Bring to the boil, then lower the heat and simmer for about half an hour.
3   Meanwhile, chop the tofu into small dice and deep-fry in the oil until golden. Drain well and set aside.
4   Mix the soya (soy) milk and flour together.
5   Pour half the contents of the saucepan into a liquidizer and blend thoroughly. Return to the saucepan. Add the milk and flour mixture and stir well. Add the tofu cubes, season, heat thoroughly and serve.

Lentil and smoked tofu soup

Smoked tofu adds a new dimension to an old-fashioned lentil soup. (Note that there is no fat added to this dish.)

IMPERIAL/METRIC		AMERICAN
6 oz (170g)	smoked tofu	$^3/_4$ cup
2 cloves	garlic	2 cloves
1$^1/_2$ pints (850ml)	water	3$^3/_4$ cups
4 oz (115g)	red lentils	$^3/_4$ cup
2	cloves	2
2 tbs	chopped parsley	2 tbs
$^3/_4$ lb (340g)	potatoes	$^3/_4$ lb
as required	freshly ground black pepper	as required
as required	sea salt (optional)	as required

1 Dice the tofu finely. Crush the garlic.
2 Put the water, lentils, tofu, garlic, cloves and parsley in a saucepan and bring to the boil.
3 Scrape or peel the potatoes and dice them very finely. Add them to the saucepan. Lower the heat, cover the saucepan, and simmer for about 20 minutes, by which time both lentils and potatoes should be very soft. Add pepper to taste (salt should not be necessary, but add a little sea salt if it is). Serve immediately.

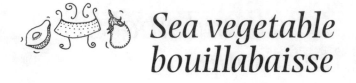 # Sea vegetable bouillabaisse

This is almost a stew rather than a soup, and I serve it with wedges of wholewheat bread. Frozen tofu adds texture and protein, while the flavour comes from the mixture of sea vegetables. As the sea vegetables expand so greatly it would be easy to make large quantities of this; just quadruple the ingredients.

IMPERIAL/METRIC		AMERICAN
$^1/_2$ oz (15g)	wakame	$^1/_2$ oz
$^1/_4$ oz (7g)	kombu	$^1/_4$ oz
$^1/_2$ oz (15g)	arame	$^1/_2$ oz
6–8 oz (170–225g)	frozen tofu	$^3/_4$–1 cup
1 small	onion	1 small
1	leek	1
2 tbs	vegetable oil	2 tbs
1 tin (about 14 oz [400g])	tomatoes	1 can (14–16 oz)
2	bay leaves	2
1 tbs	soy sauce	1 tbs

1   Put the wakame and kombu in a bowl and cover with $^3/_4$ pint (425ml, 2 cups) cold water. Leave to soak for 10–15 minutes.
2   Put the arame and tofu into another bowl and cover with boiling water. Cover the bowl and leave to soak for 10–15 minutes.
3   Drain the wakame and kombu, reserving the liquid. Chop them coarsely, discarding the inner stem of the wakame.
4   Drain the tofu and arame, and chop the tofu into small chunks.
5   Chop the onion and leek. Sauté in the oil in a large saucepan for 2–3 minutes. Add the tomatoes, bay leaves, wakame and kombu, arame, tofu, soy sauce, and the soaking liquid from the wakame and kombu. Bring to the boil, then lower the heat and simmer, uncovered, for about 20 minutes before serving.

Devilled tofu and celery spread

Tofu makes a terrific base for spreads and dips. This one is particularly good on toast or crispbread, but it can also be used in sandwiches. It is certainly flavourful.

IMPERIAL/METRIC		AMERICAN
1 lb (455g)	medium or firm tofu	2 cups
4 sticks	celery	4 sticks
4 tbs	soya (soy)-based tartare sauce (or 'Duchesse' Sandwich Spread)	4 tbs
1/2 tsp	paprika	1/2 tsp
1 tsp	ground coriander	1 tsp
1 tsp	ground cumin	1 tsp
1 tsp	curry powder	1 tsp
3 tsp	mustard	3 tsp

1　Mash the tofu. Chop the celery finely.
2　Combine all the ingredients in a mixing bowl and chill.

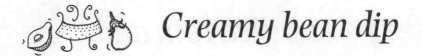

Creamy bean dip

Nothing could be quicker to make than this dip, and it is great party fare. Serve it with raw vegetables, crackers, or tortilla chips.

IMPERIAL/METRIC		AMERICAN
2 tins (about 14 oz [440g] each)	pinto beans	2 cans (14–16 oz each)
juice of 1 small or ½ large	lemon	juice of 1 small or ½ large
2 tsp	ground cumin	2 tsp
1 tsp	chilli (chili) powder	1 tsp
3–4	spring onions (scallions), chopped	3–4
½ lb (225g)	medium tofu	1 cup
2 tbs	olive oil	2 tbs
2 tsp	dried oregano	2 tsp
½ tsp	garlic salt	½ tsp

1 Drain the beans, removing some of the liquid.
2 Put all the ingredients into a liquidizer and blend, adding enough of the bean liquid to obtain the desired consistency. Chill.

Tofu guacamole 1

There are many versions of this Mexican classic, but the idea of adding tofu instead of high-fat, calorie-laden soured cream is comparatively new. The recipe below is simpler while the second one is spicy and has a more interesting texture.

IMPERIAL/METRIC		AMERICAN
1	ripe avocado	1
1 clove	garlic	1 clove
1/2 lb (225g)	medium or soft tofu	1 cup
juice of 1/2	lemon	juice of 1/2
2 tbs	vegetable oil	2 tbs
2 tsp	soy sauce	2 tsp
4 tbs	water	4 tbs

1 Peel and dice the avocado. Crush the garlic.
2 Either mash all the ingredients together or place in a liquidizer and blend. Serve immediately.

Tofu guacamole 2

This recipe is simpler and makes a smaller quantity.

IMPERIAL/METRIC		AMERICAN
$^1/_2$ lb (225g)	soft or medium tofu	1 cup
2 large	tomatoes	2 large
1 small	onion	1 small
2 cloves	garlic	2 cloves
2 fresh	chillies (chilies)	2 fresh
3	ripe avocados	3
juice of $^1/_2$	lemon	juice of $^1/_2$
as required	sea salt	as required

1 Place the tofu in a liquidizer and blend. Set aside.
2 Peel and dice the tomatoes. Chop the onion, garlic and chillies (chilies) very finely.
3 Peel and mash the avocados. Add all the rest of the ingredients and mix thoroughly. Serve immediately.

2
Salads

Valencia salad

A salad with a Mediterranean flavour. If fresh asparagus is in season it would make the dish even nicer.

IMPERIAL/METRIC		AMERICAN
³/₄ lb (340g)	brown rice	2 cups
1 small tin (about 7 oz [200g])	pimentos	1 small can (6–7 oz)
2–3 slices	onion	2–3 slices
1 tbs	chopped parsley	1 tbs
as required	sea salt	as required
¹/₃ pint (200ml)	virgin olive oil	³/₄ cup
4 tbs	cider vinegar or wine vinegar	4 tbs
1 tin (about 14 oz [400g])	artichoke hearts	1 can (14–16 oz)
¹/₂ lb (225g)	firm tofu	1 cup
1 tin (about 14 oz [400g])	asparagus	1 can (14–16 oz)

1 Cook the rice in salted boiling water until tender. Chop the pimentos and add to the rice.
2 Mix the onion slices, parsley and salt with the olive oil. Leave to stand for half an hour. Remove the onion slices and mix in the vinegar.
3 Stir half this vinaigrette into the rice and pimentos.
4 Chop the artichoke hearts coarsely. Marinate in the remaining vinaigrette.
5 Cut the tofu into cubes.
6 When ready to serve add the chopped artichoke hearts with their dressing to the rice, along with the cubes of tofu. Decorate with the asparagus.

Hijiki salad with tofu dressing

Hijiki (also spelled hiziki) is one of the nicest Japanese sea vegetables, and its tang is well complemented by a tofu dressing.

IMPERIAL/METRIC		AMERICAN
1¹/₂–2 oz (45–55g)	hijiki	1¹/₂–2 oz
4–6	spring onions (scallions)	4–6
1 lb (455g)	soft or medium tofu	2 cups
4 tbs	vegetable oil	4 tbs
1 tbs	cider vinegar or wine vinegar	1 tbs
1 tbs	tahini	1 tbs
3 tsp	soy sauce	3 tsp

1 Chop the hijiki with cold water and leave to soak for about 20 minutes. Drain, rinse, and cover with fresh water in a saucepan. Bring to the boil, cover the pan, then lower the heat, and simmer for about 10 minutes. Drain and rinse.
2 Chop the hijiki coarsely. Chop the spring onions (scallions) finely and put them in a bowl with the hijiki.
3 Put the tofu, oil, vinegar, tahini and soy sauce in a liquidizer and blend.
4 Add this tofu dressing to the hijiki and mix thoroughly before serving.

Shredded vegetable and brown rice salad with miso dressing

The list of ingredients may be long but this is a substantial dish, perfect for a summer's day when there are hearty appetites to satisfy but a hot meal has no appeal. Vegans who do not eat honey could use raw cane sugar or omit the sweet taste altogether.

IMPERIAL/METRIC		AMERICAN
4 oz (115g)	medium or firm tofu	1/2 cup
as required	vegetable oil for deep-frying	as required
3/4 lb (340g)	brown rice	2 cups
2 small or 1 large	potato	2 small or 1 large
2 large or 4 small	spring onions (scallions)	2 large or 4 small
1–2 cloves	garlic	1–2 cloves
2 tbs	chopped parsley	2 tbs
1/2 tsp	mustard powder	1/2 tsp
juice of 1/2	lemon	juice of 1/2
8 tbs	vegetable oil	8 tbs
3 tbs	cider vinegar or wine vinegar	3 tbs
1 tbs	miso	1 tbs
2 tbs	honey	2 tbs
3 tbs	water	3 tbs
2 small or 1 large	tomato	2 small or 1 large
1 stick	celery	1 stick
3 oz (85g)	white cabbage	1/3 cup
4 oz (115g)	raw beetroot (beet)	1/2 cup
3 oz (85g)	alfalfa sprouts	1/3 cup

1   Dice the tofu, deep-fry the cubes in the oil and set aside. Cook the brown rice and the potato, cool and set aside. (These preparations can be done in advance.)

2   Chop the spring onions (scallions) and garlic finely. Combine them with the parsley, mustard powder, lemon juice, and half the oil and vinegar; mix well

with the rice. Leave to marinate in a cool place or the refrigerator for at least an hour.

3 Combine the remaining oil and vinegar with the miso, honey and water and blend thoroughly in a liquidizer. Set aside.

4 Chop the potato, tomato, and celery. Grate the cabbage and beetroot (beet). Combine the vegetables with the alfalfa sprouts and fried tofu in a large bowl, and pour the miso dressing over. Mix thoroughly.

5 Use the marinated rice as a base and top with the vegetables and tofu in miso dressing.

Curried cauliflower and tofu salad

This salad has an unusual combination of flavours and textures.

IMPERIAL/METRIC		AMERICAN
8–10 oz (225g–285g)	firm or medium tofu	1–1¼ cups
as required	vegetable oil for deep-frying	as required
½ lb (225g)	brown rice	1⅓ cups
1 small	cauliflower	1 small
1 tbs	vegetable oil	1 tbs
1 tbs	cider vinegar or wine vinegar	1 tbs
4 tbs	soya (soy) mayonnaise	4 tbs
2 tbs	soya (soy) milk	2 tbs
1 tbs	curry powder	1 tbs
as required	sea salt	as required
as required	freshly ground black pepper	as required
2 small	green (bell) peppers	2 small
2 sticks	celery	2 sticks
1 small	onion	1 small
as required	lettuce	as required

1 Cube the tofu and deep-fry in the oil. Cook the rice in salted boiling water. Cool both and set aside. (These preparations may be done in advance if desired.)
2 Wash and dry the cauliflower and divide it into florets. Mix the rice with the oil, vinegar and cauliflower and set aside.
3 Combine the mayonnaise, milk, curry powder, salt and pepper in a large bowl, add the cubes of deep-fried tofu, and mix thoroughly.
4 Slice the green (bell) peppers into thin strips. Chop the celery and onion finely.
5 Combine the rice mixture, the tofu mixture, and the chopped vegetables, and serve on a bed of lettuce.

Brown rice and sweetcorn (corn) salad

Mediterranean flavours predominate in this salad, which has mashed tofu mixed into it.

IMPERIAL/METRIC		AMERICAN
½ lb (225g)	brown rice	1⅓ cups
1	green or red (bell) pepper	1
2 large or 4 small	spring onions (scallions)	2 large or 4 small
8	black olives	8
1 tin (about 14 oz [400g])	sweetcorn (corn)	1 can (14–16 oz)
2 tsp dried or 2 tbs fresh	basil	2 tsp dried or 2 tbs fresh
½ lb (225g)	firm or medium tofu	1 cup
2 tsp	soy sauce	2 tsp
½ tsp	mustard powder	½ tsp
2 tbs	cider vinegar or wine vinegar	2 tbs
2 tbs	lemon juice	2 tbs
4 tbs	virgin olive oil	4 tbs
as required	freshly ground black pepper	as required
1–2	tomatoes	1–2
as required	lettuce	as required

1 Cook the rice in salted boiling water until tender, then cool.
2 Chop the pepper. Chop the spring onions (scallions) and olives finely. Drain the sweetcorn (corn) and add it to the rice with the pepper and spring onions (scallions), olives and basil. Crumble the tofu into this mixture.
3 Combine the soy sauce, mustard powder, vinegar, lemon juice, oil and black pepper, and stir well with a fork.
4 Add this dressing to the rice and mix thoroughly. Leave for at least an hour in a cool place or the refrigerator.
5 Slice the tomatoes. Serve the salad piled on to lettuce leaves and top with the sliced tomatoes.

Rice and bulgur wheat salad with tofu dressing

Soy sauce and sesame oil (available at all Oriental stores and an increasing number of supermarkets) add a Far Eastern flavour to this salad, in which two different grains are complemented by a creamy dressing.

IMPERIAL/METRIC		AMERICAN
6 oz (170g)	brown rice	1 cup
1	onion	1
2 tbs	vegetable oil	2 tbs
1 pint (570ml)	vegetable stock	2$^1/_2$ cups
2 tsp	soy sauce	2 tsp
2 cloves	garlic	2 cloves
4 oz (115g)	bulgur wheat	$^2/_3$ cup
2 tbs	lemon juice	2 tbs
as required	sea salt	as required
$^3/_4$ lb (340g)	soft or medium tofu	1$^1/_2$ cups
2 tbs	cider vinegar or wine vinegar	2 tbs
1 tbs	sesame oil	1 tbs
2 tbs	soy sauce	2 tbs
2 tbs	chopped parsley	2 tbs
3–4	spring onions (scallions)	3–4
as required	lettuce	as required

1   Cover the rice with boiling water, cover, and leave to soak for several hours. Drain.
2   Chop the onion finely. Sauté in the vegetable oil until lightly browned. Stir in the rice, add the stock and soy sauce, bring to the boil, and simmer for 10–15 minutes.
3   Crush the garlic. Add the bulgur wheat, lemon juice, garlic and salt to the rice and simmer for about 10 minutes longer, until both rice and wheat are tender and the liquid is absorbed.

4   Put the tofu, vinegar, sesame oil, soy sauce and chopped parsley into a

liquidizer and blend thoroughly. Chop the spring onions (scallions) finely and stir into the dressing.

5 Pour the dressing over the rice and wheat, and stir well. Leave to cool, then chill in the refrigerator, and serve piled on lettuce leaves.

 # Creamy brown rice salad with marinated vegetables

As with most of the dishes in this chapter this recipe does need advance preparation, but nothing could be more appealing for a summer luncheon.

IMPERIAL/METRIC		AMERICAN
10 oz (285g)	brown rice	1²/₃ cups
¹/₂ lb (225g)	fresh or frozen green beans	¹/₂ lb
2	carrots	2
2–3	courgettes (zucchini)	2–3
2 fl oz (60ml)	virgin olive oil	¹/₄ cup
2 tbs	cider vinegar or wine vinegar	2 tbs
¹/₄ tsp	mustard powder	¹/₄ tsp
as required	sea salt	as required
as required	freshly ground black pepper	as required
1 small	onion	1 small
6 oz (170g)	medium or soft tofu	³/₄ cup
¹/₃ pint (200ml)	soya (soy) yogurt	³/₄ cup
2 cloves	garlic	2 cloves
juice of ¹/₂	lemon	juice of ¹/₂

1 Cook the rice in salted boiling water until tender then leave to cool.

2 Slice the green beans thinly and boil until just tender. Drain. Dice the carrots and courgettes (zucchini).
3 Combine the oil, vinegar, mustard powder and a little salt and pepper in a bowl. Chop the onion finely and add it to this mixture, along with the beans, courgettes (zucchini) and carrots. Mix thoroughly, cover and refrigerate for several hours.
4 Put the tofu, yogurt, garlic, and lemon juice in a liquidizer and blend thoroughly. Add salt and pepper to taste.
5 Combine the rice with the tofu mixture. Put it on a serving platter (or individual plates) and top with the vegetable mixture.

 # Brown rice, tofu and green (bell) pepper salad

A really quick and easy dish – especially if the rice has been cooked in advance and refrigerated.

IMPERIAL/METRIC		AMERICAN
10 oz (285g)	brown rice	$1^2/_3$ cups
10–12 oz (285g–340g)	firm or medium tofu	$1^1/_4$–$1^1/_2$ cups
4	spring onions (scallions)	4
1 large	green (bell) pepper	1 large
2 tbs	chopped parsley	2 tbs
4 tbs	vegetable oil	4 tbs
2 tbs	lemon juice or cider vinegar	2 tbs
$^1/_2$ tsp	garlic salt	$^1/_2$ tsp
as required	lettuce	as required
as required	sliced tomatoes	as required

1 Cook the rice in salted boiling water until tender then leave to cool.
2 Mash the tofu. Chop the spring onions (scallions) finely. Slice the green (bell)

pepper thinly. Add these ingredients to the rice together with the parsley and mix well.

3   Combine the oil, lemon juice or vinegar and garlic salt, and add to the rice mixture, stirring in thoroughly.

4   Serve on lettuce leaves, garnished with sliced tomatoes.

 # Potato salad with tofu dressing

This needs to be prepared in advance, but it takes very little time. It's a good dish for a buffet (especially for those still sceptical about non-dairy foods).

IMPERIAL/METRIC		AMERICAN
1$^{1}/_{2}$–2 lb (680–900g)	potatoes	1$^{1}/_{2}$–2 lb
8–10 oz (225g–285g)	medium or soft tofu	1–1$^{1}/_{4}$ cups
1–2 tbs	lemon juice or cider vinegar	1–2 tbs
2 tbs	vegetable oil	2 tbs
as required	sea salt	as required
as required	freshly ground black pepper	as required
1 large	onion	1 large

1   Cook the potatoes in salted boiling water until tender, drain, then peel if desired. Slice them.

2   Put the tofu, lemon juice or vinegar, oil and seasoning in a liquidizer and blend thoroughly.

3   Chop the onion finely.

4   While the potatoes are still warm mix with the onion and dressing.

5   Chill before serving.

Tofu and vegetable salad

This recipe was originally conceived as a filling for pitta bread pockets, but it can be eaten on its own too. If all the ingredients are chilled beforehand it can be served immediately.

IMPERIAL/METRIC		AMERICAN
1 lb (455g)	firm tofu	2 cups
3	spring onions (scallions)	3
1	green (bell) pepper	1
2 sticks	celery	2 sticks
1	carrot	1
6 tbs	soya (soy) mayonnaise	6 tbs

1 Cut the tofu into small cubes. Chop the spring onions (scallions), green (bell) pepper and celery finely. Grate the carrot coarsely.

2 Combine the vegetables and tofu in a bowl and stir in the mayonnaise. Chill before serving.

3
British- and American-style Dishes

Baked stuffed aubergines (eggplants)

This is an elegant dish, fit for a dinner party. Serve it with a mixed salad (and potatoes if desired).

IMPERIAL/METRIC		AMERICAN
2 large or 4 small	aubergines (eggplants)	2 large or 4 small
as required	sea salt	as required
4 tbs	olive oil	4 tbs
1	onion	1
1 clove	garlic	1 clove
³/₄ lb (340g)	mushrooms	6 cups
1 oz (30g)	vegetable margarine	2 tbs
as required	freshly ground black pepper	as required
6 oz (170g)	firm tofu	³/₄ cup
2 tbs	chopped parsley	2 tbs
¹/₂ tsp	dried thyme	¹/₂ tsp
1 tin (about 14 oz [400g])	tomatoes	1 can (14–16 oz)
1–2 tsp	dried basil or marjoram	1–2 tsp

1 Slice the aubergines (eggplants) in half lengthways. With a sharp knife make cuts in the flesh to within ¹/₄ inch (0.75cm) of the skin. Sprinkle the aubergines (eggplants) with sea salt, turn them cut side down on to kitchen towels and leave for half an hour.

2 Rinse and squeeze the aubergines (eggplants) to remove as much liquid as possible and dry them. Place skin side down on a grill (broiler) pan, and sprinkle each half with a teaspoon of the olive oil. Grill (broil) under a moderate heat for about 10 minutes until the flesh is soft.

3 Scoop the flesh from the aubergines (eggplants), leaving the skins intact. Roughly chop it and set it aside.

4   Chop the onion finely and crush the garlic. Heat the remaining olive oil in a large frying pan over a moderate heat. Add the onion and garlic and sauté for a few minutes until the onion is tender but not brown.

5   Chop the mushrooms. Add the margarine to the frying pan, and when it has melted add the mushrooms. Cook for a few more minutes, until the mushrooms are tender.

6   Remove the pan from the heat. Stir in the chopped aubergine (eggplant) flesh and black pepper to taste. Crumble the tofu into the mixture then add the parsley and thyme. Mix well.

7   Fill the aubergine (eggplant) skins with the tofu and mushroom mixture. Place them in an oiled baking dish and cover it tightly with foil. Bake in the oven at 400°F (200°C, Gas Mark 6) for 25 minutes. Uncover and bake for a further 5 minutes.

8   Meanwhile blend the tomatoes with the basil or marjoram in a liquidizer, and heat in a small saucepan. Serve the aubergines (eggplants) with the tomato sauce poured over them.

 # Tofu à la king

A quick lunch or supper dish; for one person just use a quarter of the ingredients. Serve on toast for lunch or with noodles for supper.

IMPERIAL/METRIC		AMERICAN
1/2 lb (225g)	mushrooms	4 cups
1	green (bell) pepper	1
1–1 1/4 lb (455–565g)	firm tofu	2–2 1/2 cups
4 oz (115g)	vegetable margarine	1/2 cup
3 tbs	wholemeal flour	3 tbs
1 1/4 pints (690ml)	soya (soy) milk	3 1/4 cups
as required	sea salt	as required
as required	freshly ground black pepper	as required
as required	paprika or nutmeg	as required

1   Slice the mushrooms. Chop the green (bell) pepper. Cut the tofu into cubes.
2   Melt the margarine in a saucepan and fry the mushrooms and green pepper until soft. Stir in the flour and cook for 2–3 minutes. Add the milk very gradually, stirring constantly, bring to the boil and continue stirring until thickened. Add the tofu and season to taste with salt, pepper and the paprika or nutmeg.

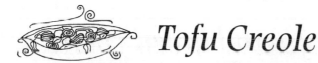

Tofu Creole

Another quick and easy dish, especially if the tofu cubes are deep-fried in advance. It is good served with brown rice or pasta.

IMPERIAL/METRIC		AMERICAN
1 lb (455g)	firm tofu	2 cups
as required	vegetable oil for deep-frying	as required
2 small or 1 large	onion	2 small or 1 large
1	green (bell) pepper	1
2 oz (55g)	vegetable margarine	$^1/_4$ cup
6 tbs	wholewheat flour	6 tbs
2 tins (about 14 oz [400g] each)	tomatoes	2 cans (14–16 oz each)
2 tsp	dried rosemary	2 tsp
2 tsp	dried thyme	2 tsp
2 tsp	dried oregano	2 tsp
2 tsp	raw cane sugar	2 tsp
as required	sea salt	as required
as required	freshly ground black pepper	as required

1 Cut the tofu into cubes and deep-fry in the oil until browned. Drain well.
2 Finely chop the onion and green (bell) pepper. Sauté gently in the margarine for a few minutes until soft. Stir in the flour and gradually add the tomatoes (chopping them coarsely as you do so) and the herbs, sugar and seasoning. Cook for 10–15 minutes until the sauce has thickened and the flavours have blended.
3 Add the tofu and cook for a further 5 minutes. Serve immediately.

Tofu and green (bell) pepper bake

This is a light lunch dish; for a more substantial meal double the quantities. Serve with wholewheat toast.

IMPERIAL/METRIC		AMERICAN
³/₄ lb (340g)	firm tofu	1¹/₂ cups
2	green (bell) peppers	2
1 clove	garlic	1 clove
1 lb (455g)	tomatoes	1 lb
1 tsp	Tabasco sauce	1 tsp
4–6 tbs	soya (soy) yogurt	4–6 tbs
2 tsp	paprika	2 tsp
as required	sea salt	as required

1 Put the tofu into a clean tea towel (dish towel) and squeeze until most of the moisture has gone. Put the dry, crumbly tofu into a mixing bowl.
2 Chop the green (bell) peppers, garlic and tomatoes.
3 Combine all the ingredients with the tofu. Put into an ovenproof dish, and bake in the oven at 400°F (200°C, Gas Mark 6) for 20 minutes.

Baked tofu squares

A pleasant family dish. Serve with a green salad or cooked green vegetables and, for a really filling meal, potatoes as well. The rice can be cooked in advance.

IMPERIAL/METRIC		AMERICAN
6 oz (170g)	short-grain brown rice	1 cup
³/₄ lb (340g)	firm tofu	1¹/₂ cups
7–8 fl oz (200–225ml)	soya (soy) milk	1 cup
2 tbs	soya (soy) flour	2 tbs
2 tsp	sea salt	2 tsp
2	onions	2
2 tbs	vegetable oil	2 tbs
2	carrots	2
1 tin (about 14 oz [400g])	kidney beans	1 can (14–16 oz)
2 tsp	dried rosemary	2 tsp

1   Cook the rice in salted boiling water then set aside.
2   Mash the tofu. Add the milk, flour and salt and mix thoroughly.
3   Chop the onions finely. Sauté in the oil until softened but not brown. Add to the tofu mixture.
4   Grate the carrots finely. Drain the beans. Add both to the tofu mixture with the rice and rosemary. Mix thoroughly.
5   Turn the mixture into an oiled ovenproof dish. Bake in the oven at 375°F (190°C, Gas Mark 5) for about 25 minutes, until the top is a light golden brown. Cool briefly before cutting it into squares.

 # Tofu casserole

In spite of the curry powder, this has no pretensions to Indian cuisine. It can be served with vegetables or salad as desired.

IMPERIAL/METRIC		AMERICAN
3 oz (85g)	vegetable margarine	¹/₃ cup
4 tbs	wholewheat flour	4 tbs
³/₄ pint (425ml)	soya (soy) milk	2 cups
³/₄–1 lb (340–455g)	firm tofu	1¹/₂–2 cups
1	onion	1
1	green (bell) pepper	1
2 tbs	vegetable oil	2 tbs
2 tsp	curry powder	2 tsp
1 tin (about 14 oz [400g])	tomatoes	1 can (14–16 oz)
as required	sea salt	as required
2 oz (55g)	dried wholewheat breadcrumbs	¹/₂ cup

1   Melt 2 oz (55g, 1/4 cup) of the margarine in a pan, stir in the flour and cook briefly for about 2 minutes. Slowly add the milk, stirring constantly, until it comes to the boil and thickens into a white sauce. Set aside.
2   Cut the tofu into cubes. Sauté in the remaining margarine until golden. Set aside.
3   Chop the onion and green (bell) pepper finely. Sauté in the vegetable oil until tender. Add the curry powder and stir briefly. Add the tomatoes and cook for about 10 minutes, stirring occasionally.
4   Add the tomato mixture and the tofu to the white sauce and mix thoroughly. Season to taste. Turn into an oiled casserole, and top with the breadcrumbs (additional margarine may be used to dot the top of the casserole if desired). Bake in an oven at 350°F (180°C, Gas Mark 4) for about 15 minutes.

Gingered potato and tofu savoury

A green salad or cooked green vegetable such as broccoli or spinach provides a good contrast of colour and flavour to this dish. The potatoes can be cooked in advance.

IMPERIAL/METRIC		AMERICAN
1½ lb (680g)	potatoes	1½ lb
2 oz (55g)	sesame seeds	⅓ cup
½ lb (225g)	firm tofu	1 cup
¼ pint (140ml)	soya (soy) milk	⅔ cup
2 tsp	cider vinegar	2 tsp
1	onion	1
1–2 inch (2.5cm) piece	fresh ginger	1–2 inch piece
3 oz (85g)	broken cashews	⅔ cup
as required	sea salt	as required

1 Cook the potatoes in salted boiling water, cool and mash them then set aside.
2 Grind the sesame seeds and set aside.
3 Put the tofu, milk and vinegar in a liquidizer and blend thoroughly.
4 Peel and chop the onion and ginger and add to the liquidizer. Blend until smooth.
5 Add this mixture to the mashed potatoes, together with the ground sesame seeds and the cashew pieces. Add sea salt to taste and mix thoroughly.
6 Put into an oiled baking dish, and bake in the oven at 350°F (180°C, Gas Mark 4) for about an hour, until the top is lightly browned.

Tofu and spaghetti casserole

A nice contrast of textures characterizes this dish. Breaking the spaghetti into two or three pieces before cooking it is a good idea.

IMPERIAL/METRIC		AMERICAN
3 tbs	vegetable margarine	3 tbs
2 tbs	wholewheat flour	2 tbs
$^1/_2$ pint (285ml)	soya (soy) milk	$1^1/_3$ cups
$^1/_2$ tsp	celery salt	$^1/_2$ tsp
1 tsp	lemon juice	1 tsp
2 tbs	chopped parsley	2 tbs
$^1/_2$ lb (225g)	firm tofu	1 cup
$^1/_2$ lb (225g)	wholewheat spaghetti	$^1/_2$ lb
6 oz (170g)	mushrooms	3 cups
1 small or $^1/_2$ large	green (bell) pepper	1 small or $^1/_2$ large
3 oz (85g)	blanched flaked (slivered) almonds	$^3/_4$ cup
2 oz (55g)	fresh breadcrumbs	1 cup

1 Melt 2 tbs of the margarine in a pan; stir in the flour, then gradually add the milk, stirring constantly until thickened. Add the celery salt, lemon juice and parsley. Crumble the tofu into the pan and stir well. Set aside.
2 Cook the spaghetti in salted boiling water until tender. Drain and set aside.
3 Chop the mushrooms. Sauté in the remaining margarine until tender. Chop the green (bell) pepper finely.
4 Add the mushrooms, green (bell) pepper and almonds to the creamed tofu mixture with the cooked spaghetti. Mix thoroughly.
5 Place in an oiled casserole, top with the breadcrumbs and bake in the oven at 375°F (190°C, Gas Mark 5) for about 20 minutes, or until the top is lightly browned.

Sweet and sour cabbage

If there were a chapter in this book for Eastern European-style recipes this one would belong there, but such dishes have long since been appropriated by the West, especially the USA. Vegans who avoid honey could substitute raw cane sugar to taste.

IMPERIAL/METRIC		AMERICAN
1 lb (455g)	cabbage	1 lb
2	onions	2
2	eating apples	2
2	lemons	2
1/2 lb (225g)	firm tofu	1 cup
1 1/2 tbs	honey	1 1/2 tbs
1/4 pint (140ml)	soya (soy) yogurt	2/3 cup
1/2 lb (225g)	bulgur wheat	1 1/3 cups
1 tbs	caraway seeds	1 tbs
2 tbs	cider vinegar	2 tbs
2 tbs	vegetable oil	2 tbs
2 oz (55g)	raisins	1/3 cup
as required	sea salt	as required
as required	freshly ground black pepper	as required
1/2 pint (285ml)	water	1 1/3 cups
pinch	allspice	pinch

1 Shred the cabbage; chop the onions; peel and dice the apples. Squeeze the lemons, retaining only the juice.
2 Crumble the tofu into a large mixing bowl. Mix in all of the rest of the ingredients.
3 Place in an oiled casserole, and bake in the oven at 400°F (200°C, Gas Mark 6) for about 10 minutes, then lower the heat to 350°F (180°C, Gas Mark 4) for a further 20 minutes.

 # Devilled tofu

This dish involves several different processes, but it is complete in itself, requiring no accompaniments.

IMPERIAL/METRIC		AMERICAN
³/₄ lb (340g)	brown rice	2 cups
1	onion	1
1 large	green (bell) pepper	1 large
2 sticks	celery	2 sticks
4 oz (115g)	vegetable margarine	¹/₂ cup
4 oz (115g)	mushrooms	2 cups
as required	vegetable stock	as required
as required	sea salt	as required
³/₄–1 lb (340–455g)	firm tofu	1¹/₂–2 cups
2 oz (55g)	wholewheat flour	¹/₂ cup
¹/₂ pint (285ml)	water	1¹/₃ cups
4 tbs	tomato purée (paste)	4 tbs
1–2 tsp	mustard	1–2 tsp

1 Cover the rice with boiling water and leave to soak for several hours. Drain and set aside.
2 Chop the onion, green (bell) pepper and celery. Sauté in a quarter of the margarine for about 5 minutes, stirring occasionally. Chop the mushrooms, add them to the pan, along with the rice, and cook gently for 3–4 minutes. Add stock to cover and a little salt, bring to the boil, cover and simmer until tender.
3 Meanwhile, cut the tofu into cubes and sauté in a quarter of the margarine for a few minutes, turning it so that it is golden on all sides. Set aside.
4 Melt the remaining margarine in a pan and stir in the flour. Cook for about 2 minutes, then carefully add the water, stirring constantly. Bring to the boil, stirring as it thickens, and add the tomato purée (paste) and mustard.
5 Turn the rice mixture into a large serving dish (or on to 4 plates). Arrange the tofu cubes on top, and pour the sauce over the whole.

 # *Savoury tofu triangles*

This combination of ingredients makes a lovely filling for pastry. Serve the triangles with a mixed salad.

IMPERIAL/METRIC		AMERICAN
	Pastry:	
10 oz (285g)	wholewheat flour	2^1/$_2$ cups
as required	sea salt	as required
5 oz (140g)	vegetable margarine	^{2}/$_3$ cup
	Filling:	
^{1}/$_2$ lb (225g)	fresh or frozen spinach	5 cups
1	onion	1
2 tbs	vegetable oil	2 tbs
4 oz (115g)	mushrooms	2 cups
3 tbs	sesame seeds	3 tbs
1–2 tbs	soy sauce	1–2 tbs
^{3}/$_4$–1 lb (340g–455g)	medium or firm tofu	1^1/$_2$–2 cups

1   To make the pastry, put the flour in a mixing bowl and add a little salt. Mix the margarine in with the fingers, a fork or a pastry blender (with a firm margarine it is easiest to use a pastry blender; with a soft margarine a fork is best). Add enough water to make a dough that is firm but not dry (it is better to have it a little sticky and use extra flour on the pastry board than to have it too dry – moister pastry at this stage makes for lighter pastry when cooked). Roll out and cut into squares (either 4 large, 8 medium or 16 small ones).

2   To make the filling, steam the spinach until tender then chop it and set aside.

3   Chop the onion and sauté in the oil until tender. Chop the mushrooms, add the onion and sauté for a further 3–4 minutes.

4   Toast the sesame seeds under a grill (broiler). Add to the onions and mushrooms along with the chopped spinach and the soy sauce.

5   Crumble the tofu into the spinach mixture.

6   Divide the filling evenly between the squares and fold them over into triangles. Put them on lightly oiled baking sheets, prick the tops with a fork, and bake in the oven at 400°F (200°C, Gas Mark 6) for about 15 minutes, until golden. Serve immediately.

Savoury tofu and bulgur wheat

This casserole would be a bit insubstantial on its own, but serving it with bulgur wheat provides a good contrast in textures and makes it into a self-contained dish.

IMPERIAL/METRIC		AMERICAN
1	onion	1
4 sticks	celery	4 sticks
2 tbs	vegetable oil	2 tbs
1 tbs	chopped parsley	1 tbs
10 oz (285g)	soft or medium tofu	1¼ cups
¼ pint (140ml)	tomato juice	⅔ cup
3 oz (85g)	walnuts	⅔ cup
2 oz (55g)	wholewheat breadcrumbs	1 cup
2 tbs	dried potato flakes or instant mashed potato	2 tbs
1 tsp	lemon juice	1 tsp
½ tsp	dried thyme	½ tsp
½ lb (225g)	bulgur wheat	1⅓ cups
as required	sea salt	as required

1 Chop the onion and celery finely. Sauté in the oil until softened but not brown. Add the parsley.
2 Mash the tofu and mix with the tomato juice. Chop the walnuts finely and add to the tofu mixture with the breadcrumbs and dried potato. Mix well.
3 Add the sautéed vegetables, and lemon juice and thyme to the tofu and mix thoroughly. Place the mixture in an oiled casserole. Bake at 350°F (180°C, Gas Mark 4) for 40 minutes.
4 Meanwhile, cook the bulgur wheat (use treble the amount of water to bulgur wheat) with a little sea salt until tender.
5 Serve the tofu casserole with the wheat.

Quick and easy shepherd's pie

A traditional English dish with a new ingredient. The potatoes can be freshly cooked or cooked in advance, and mashed with soya (soy) milk, vegetable margarine and seasoning, or an instant mashed potato mix may be used. Serve with cooked vegetables.

IMPERIAL/METRIC		AMERICAN
2	onions	2
4 tbs	vegetable oil	4 tbs
3 tbs	flour	3 tbs
½ pint (285ml)	water	1⅓ cups
1 tbs	yeast extract	1 tbs
1 lb (455g)	medium or firm tofu	2 cups
1 lb (455g)	mashed potatoes	1 lb

1 Chop the onions and sauté in the oil until lightly browned.
2 Stir in the flour, then gradually add the water, stirring constantly. When boiling and thickened, turn the heat down and stir in the yeast extract.
3 Crumble the tofu into the saucepan, and mix well. Turn into an oiled casserole and top with the mashed potatoes.
4 Bake in the oven at 375°F (190°C, Gas Mark 5) for 15–20 minutes until the top is lightly browned.

Shepherd's pie with vegetables

A more elaborate version of this old favourite than the one above. Although it takes longer to prepare it does not need any accompanying vegetables.

IMPERIAL/METRIC		AMERICAN
1	onion	1
2 tbs	vegetable oil	2 tbs
4 oz (115g)	mushrooms	2 cups
1	green (bell) pepper	1
2	carrots	2
1 tin (about 14 oz [400g])	tomatoes	1 can (14–16 oz)
1	bay leaf	1
$^1/_2$ tsp	dried basil	$^1/_2$ tsp
1 lb (455g)	medium or firm tofu	2 cups
1 lb (455g)	mashed potatoes	1 lb

1 Chop the onion and sauté in the oil until just tender.
2 Chop the mushrooms, green (bell) pepper and carrots. Add to the onion and stir well.
3 Add the tomatoes, bay leaf and basil. Cover and simmer for about 10 minutes. Crumble the tofu into the mixture and cook for a further 5 minutes.
4 Turn into a greased casserole, cover with the mashed potatoes, and bake in the oven at 375°F (190°C, Gas Mark 5) for 15–20 minutes until lightly browned.

Tofu burgers are now readily available in health-food stores, and even supermarkets, but they are never as good as the homemade kind. There are innumerable combinations of ingredients which can be used to make tofu burgers, and here are two examples. The first makes four small burgers for a light lunch; the second makes up to eight burgers depending on size. Serve them in a bun with lettuce or alfalfa sprouts and tomato ketchup or sliced tomatoes, or alternatively with gravy and vegetables.

 # Tofu burgers 1

IMPERIAL/METRIC		AMERICAN
2	onions	2
3 sticks	celery	3 sticks
2 tbs plus additional for frying	vegetable oil	2 tbs plus additional for frying
1–1½ lb (455–680g)	firm tofu	2–3 cups
4 oz (115g)	rolled oats	1 cup
2 tbs	soy sauce	2 tbs
1 tsp	garlic salt	1 tsp

1 Chop the onions and celery finely. Sauté in the 2 tbs oil until lightly browned.
2 Crumble or mash the tofu in a bowl. Add the oats, soy sauce, garlic salt, and the sautéed onion and celery. Mix well and knead with the hands. Form into burgers and shallow-fry until browned on both sides.

 *Tofu burgers 2*

IMPERIAL/METRIC		AMERICAN
$^1/_2$ lb (225g)	firm tofu	1 cup
2 oz (55g)	sunflower seeds	$^1/_2$ cup
2 oz (55g)	wholewheat breadcrumbs	1 cup
$^3/_4$ tsp	onion salt	$^3/_4$ tsp
$^3/_4$ tsp	garlic salt	$^3/_4$ tsp
3–4 tbs	soy sauce	3–4 tbs
as required	vegetable oil for frying	as required

1 Drain the tofu well and mash in a bowl.
2 Grind the sunflower seeds.
3 Add the sunflower seeds, breadcrumbs, salts and soy sauce to the tofu and mix well. Form into 4 burgers.
4 Shallow-fry in a little oil until browned on both sides.

Tofu pot pie

If shepherd's pie is the traditional English winter dish, then pot pie is the American equivalent. Here is a new version. For hints on making wholewheat pastry see the recipe for Savoury tofu triangles on p. 41.

IMPERIAL/METRIC		AMERICAN
1 lb (455g)	firm tofu	2 cups
2 oz (55g) plus	wholewheat flour	¹/₂ cup plus
3 tbs		3 tbs
2 tsp	garlic salt	2 tsp
6 tbs	vegetable oil	6 tbs
2 small	carrots	2 small
3 sticks	celery	3 sticks
1	large onion	1
4 oz (115g)	fresh (shelled) or frozen peas	²/₃ cup
³/₄ pint (425ml)	soya (soy) milk	2 cups
as required	sea salt	as required
as required	freshly ground black pepper	as required
1 tsp	dried sage	1 tsp
¹/₂ tsp	dried thyme	¹/₂ tsp
1 tsp	paprika	1 tsp

1 Make the pastry and divide into 2 portions, one larger than the other. Roll out the larger portion, put it into a pie dish, prick with a fork, and bake in the oven at 400°F (200°C, Gas Mark 6) for 10 minutes.

2 Cut the tofu into cubes. Combine the 2 oz (55g, 1/2 cup) flour with the garlic salt. Toss the tofu cubes in this mixture.

3 Heat 4 tablespoons of the oil in a frying pan and add the coated tofu cubes. Stir well over a medium heat until browned.

4 Chop the carrots, celery and onion and add to the tofu. Stir-fry until just tender. Add the peas and stir-fry for another minute or two.

5 Heat the remaining oil in a saucepan. Gradually stir in the 3 tbs flour, then the milk, stirring constantly to avoid lumps. When this has come to the boil add the salt, pepper, sage, thyme and paprika.

6 Combine the sauce with the tofu and vegetable mixture and pour into the pie shell. Put the top crust over it, prick with a fork, and bake in the oven at 375°F (190°C, Gas Mark 5) for about half an hour until lightly browned.

 # Grilled tofu with gravy

This is a pleasant dish for a light lunch, and is simple to make for just one person (use a quarter of the ingredients).

IMPERIAL/METRIC		AMERICAN
1 lb (455g)	firm tofu	2 cups
as required	soy sauce	as required
¹/₂ pint (285ml)	water	1¹/₃ cups
3 tbs	tahini	3 tbs
2 heaped tsp	miso	3 heaped tsp
10–12 slices	wholewheat bread	10–12 slices
as required	vegetable margarine (optional)	as required

1 Cut the tofu into slices about 1/2 inch (1.25 cm) thick. Place the slices on a grill (broiler) pan and brush the tops with a little soy sauce. Grill (broil) under medium heat for a few minutes. Turn the slices over, brush with a little more soy sauce, and grill the other side.
2 Meanwhile, bring the water to the boil. Put the tahini and miso into a liquidizer, add the water, and blend. Pour this sauce into a pan, bring to the boil over a low heat, simmer for 1–2 minutes, then leave to rest for 2–3 minutes.
3 Toast the bread, place the tofu slices on top (spread the toast with vegetable margarine if desired), and spoon the gravy over them.

'Cheesy' mushroom scramble

Another light lunch dish that can easily be adapted for one person; use a quarter of the ingredients.

IMPERIAL/METRIC		AMERICAN
4 oz (115g)	vegetable margarine	1/2 cup
2 oz (55g)	soya (soy) flour	1/2 cup
1 1/2–2 tsp	yeast extract	1 1/2–2 tsp
1	onion	1
3/4 lb (340g)	mushrooms	6 cups
4 oz (115g)	fresh (shelled) or frozen peas	7/3 cup
1/2 lb (225g)	firm tofu	1 cup
as required	wholewheat toast	as required

1 Melt 3 oz (85g, 1/3 cup) of the margarine in a pan. Remove from the heat and stir in the soya (soy) flour and yeast extract. Spoon on to an oiled flat surface and leave to cool, then chill. (This is the 'cheese'.)

2 Chop the onion and sauté in the remaining margarine in a large frying pan until just tender.

3 Slice the mushrooms and add to the frying pan. Stir-fry for 2–3 minutes, then add the peas and cook for a few minutes longer.

4 Crumble the tofu into the frying pan and continue cooking 3–4 minutes longer.

5 Cut the chilled 'cheese' into small pieces and add to the frying pan, stirring well while it melts. Cook for a further 2–3 minutes, then serve on toast.

Tofu roast

There is nothing quite like a roast – served with gravy and vegetables – for a cold winter evening. This one is highly nutritious and undeniably different.

IMPERIAL/METRIC		AMERICAN
1	onion	1
2 tbs	vegetable oil	2 tbs
6 oz (170g)	brown rice	1 cup
6 oz (170g)	red lentils	1 cup
2 tsp	yeast extract	2 tsp
2 oz (55g)	wholewheat breadcrumbs	1 cup
½ lb (225g)	medium or firm tofu	1 cup
1 small tin (7 oz [200g])	tomatoes	1 can (7–8 oz)

1 Chop the onion finely and sauté in the oil until lightly browned.
2 Cook the rice and lentils in salted boiling water until tender. They can be cooked together in the same pan if the rice has been well soaked beforehand.
3 Add the cooked rice and lentils to the onion, along with the yeast extract and breadcrumbs. Crumble or mash the tofu and add to this mixture.
4 Blend the tomatoes in a liquidizer and slowly mix in. The mixture should be moist but firm; do not add all the tomatoes if it looks like becoming too sloppy.
5 Put into a baking dish and bake in the oven at 350°F (180°C, Gas Mark 4) for about 40 minutes, until nicely browned.

Vegetables topped with tofu custard

An unusual and tasty mixture. Serve with boiled, roast or baked potatoes.

IMPERIAL/METRIC		AMERICAN
1 lb (455g)	frozen chopped spinach	1 lb
³/₄ lb (340g)	hard white cabbage	³/₄ lb
2	leeks	2
4 tbs	vegetable oil	4 tbs
4 small or 3 large	courgettes (zucchini)	4 small or 3 large
2 cloves	garlic	2 cloves
as required	sea salt	as required
1¹/₄–1¹/₂ lb (565–680g)	medium tofu	2¹/₂–2 cups
3 tbs	tahini	3 tbs
juice of 1	lemon	juice of 1
3 tsp	soy sauce	3 tsp
4 tbs	soya (soy) yogurt	4 tbs
¹/₂ tsp	cayenne pepper (optional)	¹/₂ tsp
2 oz (55g)	wholewheat breadcrumbs	1 cup

1 Cook the spinach until tender.
2 Chop the cabbage and leeks. Put them in a wok or large frying pan with the oil. Stir-fry for 1–2 minutes, then cover, lower the heat, and cook for 4–5 minutes.
3 Chop the courgettes (zucchini) coarsely. Chop the garlic finely. Add to the pan and stir-fry for 4–5 minutes longer. Add the spinach and salt to taste.
4 Combine the tofu, tahini, lemon juice, soy sauce, yogurt and cayenne pepper (if used) in a liquidizer and blend until smooth.
5 Put the vegetables into an oiled casserole dish and pour the tofu mixture over them. Top with the breadcrumbs. Bake in the oven at 350°F (180°C, Gas Mark 4) for 35 minutes.

Cauliflower terrine

An elegant dish. Serve with fried or roast potatoes, and with a mixed salad if desired.

IMPERIAL/METRIC		AMERICAN
1 large	cauliflower	1 large
2	onions	2
2 tbs	vegetable oil	2 tbs
10–12 oz (285–340g)	medium tofu	1¼–1½ cups
4 tbs	soya (soy) yogurt	4 tbs
4 tbs	tahini	4 tbs
juice of 1	lemon	juice of 1
6 oz (170g)	wholewheat breadcrumbs	3 cups
pinch	grated nutmeg	pinch
6–8 tbs	Smokey Snaps (soy bakon bits)	6–8 tbs
as required	sea salt	as required
2 tbs	chopped parsley	2 tbs

1 Divide the cauliflower into florets and cook in salted boiling water until tender. Drain then mash into a purée.
2 Chop the onions and sauté in the oil until tender but not brown.
3 Put the tofu, yogurt, tahini and lemon juice in a liquidizer and blend thoroughly.
4 Combine all of the ingredients, and put into an oiled casserole or loaf tin. Bake in the oven at 375°F (190°C, Gas Mark 5) for 1 hour.

Cauliflower with tangy tomato/tofu topping

This is another baked cauliflower dish, this time with the creamy tofu mixture as a separate layer. Serve with boiled, baked or roast potatoes.

IMPERIAL/METRIC		AMERICAN
1 large	cauliflower	1 large
1 large	onion	1 large
1 oz (30g)	vegetable margarine	2 tbs
1¹/₂ lb (680g)	medium tofu	3 cups
1 tbs	vegetable oil	1 tbs
3 tsp	mustard	3 tsp
3 tbs	tomato purée (paste)	3 tbs
as required	sea salt	as required
as required	freshly ground black pepper	as required
4 tbs	chopped parsley	4 tbs

1   Break the cauliflower into florets. Steam in a little salted water until just tender. Drain.
2   Chop the onion and sauté in the margarine until lightly browned.
3   Put the tofu, oil and mustard, tomato purée (paste) and seasoning in a liquidizer and blend thoroughly. Stir in the parsley and fried onion into this mixture.
4   Put the cauliflower into a greased ovenproof dish and pour the tofu mixture over. Bake in the oven at 400°F (200°C, Gas Mark 6) for half an hour.

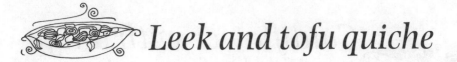

Leek and tofu quiche

Who says a quiche has to have cheese or eggs in it? Serve it hot or cold with salad.

IMPERIAL/METRIC		AMERICAN
2 large	leeks	2 large
1 oz (30g)	vegetable margarine	2 tbs
1–1½ lb (455–680g)	medium tofu	2–3 cups
2 tbs	lemon juice	2 tbs
1 tsp	garlic salt	1 tsp
as required	freshly ground black pepper	as required
	uncooked wholewheat pastry shell (made from 6–8 oz [170–225g, 1½–2 cups] flour and 3–4 oz [85–115g, ⅓–½ cup] vegetable margarine)	

1 Wash and slice the leeks. Sauté in the margarine for 3–4 minutes.
2 Mash the tofu in a mixing bowl. Stir in the lemon juice, garlic salt and black pepper. Add the sautéed leeks and mix in well.
3 Pour the filling into the pastry shell.
4 Bake in the oven at 400°F (200°C, Gas Mark 6) for about half an hour, until set and lightly browned.

Savoury tofu cutlets

When tofu has been frozen it acquires a chewy texture, which makes it ideal for cutlets. Serve hot – for a main meal with potatoes and seasonal vegetables, or for a light lunch with salad.

IMPERIAL/METRIC		AMERICAN
1–1¼ lb (455–565g)	firm tofu (cut into 12 slices and frozen)	2–2½ cups
6 tbs	soy sauce	6 tbs
2 tbs	water	2 tbs
1 tbs	cider vinegar	1 tbs
1 clove	garlic	1 clove
as required	freshly ground black pepper	as required
as required	wholewheat flour	as required
as required	vegetable oil	as required

1 Defrost and gently squeeze the tofu slices.
2 Combine the soy sauce, water and vinegar in a bowl. Crush the garlic and add it to the bowl with some black pepper. Mix well. Turn the tofu slices in this mixture until they are saturated.
3 Spread some flour out on a plate and turn the tofu slices in it so that they are well coated on both sides.
4 Heat a little oil in a frying pan, and fry the slices, turning them once so they are nicely browned on both sides.

Smoked tofu turnovers

Smoked tofu adds a new dimension to savoury dishes. These turnovers can be served hot with vegetables or cold with salad.

IMPERIAL/METRIC		AMERICAN
	Filling:	
6–8 oz (170–225g)	potatoes	6–8 oz
1 large or 2 small	leeks	1 large or 2 small
2 tbs	vegetable oil	2 tbs
10 oz (285g)	smoked tofu	1$^{1}/_{4}$ cups
as required	sea salt	as required
as required	freshly ground black pepper	as required
	Pastry:	
10 oz (285g)	wholewheat flour	2$^{1}/_{2}$ cups
pinch	sea salt	pinch
$^{1}/_{2}$ tsp	baking powder	$^{1}/_{2}$ tsp
5 oz (140g)	vegetable margarine	$^{2}/_{3}$ cup

1 Cook the potatoes in salted boiling water (or use leftover cooked potatoes) and dice them.
2 Chop the leeks finely. Heat the oil in a frying pan and sauté the leeks for 2–3 minutes. Chop the tofu into small dice, add them to the pan and sauté for a further 3 minutes or so, stirring frequently. Add the potato and season to taste.
3 Combine the flour, salt and baking powder in a large bowl. Mix in the margarine with a pastry blender or fork, then slowly add enough water to make a moist dough. Roll out, and cut into 8 or 16 rounds.
4 Spoon the filling into the centre of the rounds, then gather up the edges of the dough and pinch together at the top. Place the turnovers on an oiled baking tray and bake in the oven at 400°F (200°C, Gas Mark 6) for about 25 minutes.

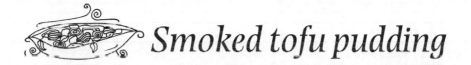

Smoked tofu pudding

This is an ideal dish for a cold winter evening. Serve it with a vegetarian gravy and seasonal vegetables.

IMPERIAL/METRIC		AMERICAN
1 lb (455g)	potatoes	1 lb
2 cans (about 14 oz [400g] each)	haricot (navy) beans	2 cans (14–16 oz each)
10 oz (285g)	smoked tofu	1 1/4 cups
2 tbs	vegetable oil	2 tbs
2 tsp	dried sage	2 tsp
as required	sea salt	as required
as required	freshly ground black pepper	as required

1 Cook the potatoes in salted boiling water (or use leftover cooked potatoes). Drain and rinse the haricot (navy) beans.
2 Chop the smoked tofu finely. Sauté it in the vegetable oil for about 3 minutes.
3 Mash the potatoes and the beans. Mix the sautéed tofu in and add the sage and seasoning. Transfer to a baking dish and bake in the oven at 375°F (190°C, Gas Mark 5) for about 45 minutes.

# Steamed smoked tofu pudding

Another winter dish – this time steamed instead of baked. Serve it with a tomato sauce, either a good-quality proprietary sauce or a homemade one (the quickest homemade sauce is simply a can of tomatoes liquidized with herbs and seasonings to taste) and with seasonal vegetables.

IMPERIAL/METRIC		AMERICAN
1/2 lb (225g)	wholewheat flour	2 cups
3 tsp	baking powder	3 tsp
1 tsp	sea salt	1 tsp
4 oz (115g)	hard vegetable fat	1/2 cup
1/2 lb (225g)	smoked tofu	1 cup
2	onions	2
1 small tin (about 6 oz [170g])	tomatoes	1 can (about 7 oz)
1 tsp	dried sage	1 tsp

1 Mix the flour, baking powder and salt in a large bowl. Grate the fat and mix it in. Add enough water to make a dough, roll out about two-thirds of it, then use to line a large, greased pudding bowl.
2 Dice the smoked tofu. Chop the onions. Remove the tomatoes from the can (the juice can be kept for the sauce if desired) and chop them coarsely. Combine these ingredients in a bowl and stir in the sage. Spoon this mixture into the pastry-lined pudding bowl.
3 Roll out the remaining third of the pastry to make a lid and fit it over the tofu mixture. Cover the bowl with foil and place in a large saucepan of boiling water. Lower the heat and steam for about 2 hours.

Smoked tofu charlotte

This is a simple, tasty dish. Serve with boiled or baked potatoes.

IMPERIAL/METRIC		AMERICAN
6 oz (170g)	smoked tofu	³/₄ cup
2 tbs	vegetable oil	2 tbs
¹/₂ lb (225g)	mushrooms	4 cups
5 sticks	celery	5 sticks
2¹/₂ oz (170g)	vegetable margarine	¹/₄ cup plus 1 tbs
2 oz (55g)	wholewheat flour	¹/₂ cup
³/₄ pint (425ml)	soya (soy) milk	2 cups
as required	sea salt	as required
as required	freshly ground black pepper	as required
4 oz (115g)	wholewheat breadcrumbs	2 cups

1 Dice the smoked tofu and sauté in the oil in a frying pan for a few minutes. Set aside.
2 Chop the mushrooms and celery. Sauté them in a separate pan in 2 oz (55g, 1/4 cup) of the margarine for a few minutes.
3 Stir the flour into the mushrooms and celery, cook for about a minute, then gradually stir in the milk. Stir until thickened, then season. Stir in the tofu.
4 Transfer to a greased baking dish and top with the breadcrumbs. Bake in the oven at 350°F (190°C, Gas Mark 5) for 15–20 minutes, and serve hot.

4
Mexican-style dishes

Chili con tofu 1

Tofu adds the texture of mince to chilli (chili) dishes. This one can be served with rice or us a filling for tacos. (NB. Chilli powder is not the same as Mexican chili seasoning, which can be found at most supermarkets.)

IMPERIAL/METRIC		AMERICAN
2	onions	2
2 tbs	vegetable oil	2 tbs
2 tins (about 14 oz [400g each])	kidney beans	2 cans (14–16 oz each)
½ lb (225g)	firm tofu	1 cup
as required	Mexican chili seasoning	as required
5 oz (140g)	tomato purée (paste)	⅔ cup
4 oz (115g)	wholewheat breadcrumbs	2 cups

1 Chop the onions and fry in the oil until lightly browned. Drain the kidney beans.
2 Put the tofu into a clean tea towel (dish towel) and squeeze as much of the liquid out as possible so that the tofu is quite dry and crumbly.
3 Combine all of the ingredients in a saucepan, adding enough water to make the mixture stirrable. Bring to the boil over a moderate heat, stirring constantly; turn the heat to low and simmer for about 10 minutes.

Chili con tofu 2

Frozen tofu is even more 'meaty' than fresh. This recipe was created as a filling for pitta bread, but it could as easily be served with rice or tortilla chips.

IMPERIAL/METRIC		AMERICAN
¹/₂ lb (225g)	frozen tofu	1 cup
2	onions	2
2 tbs	vegetable oil	2 tbs
1	carrot	1
1 stick	celery	1 stick
1 small	green (bell) pepper	1 small
1 clove	garlic	1 clove
¹/₂ lb (225g)	mushrooms	4 cups
4	tomatoes	4 small
1 lb (455g)	drained cooked kidney beans	1 lb
2 tbs	water	2 tbs
2 tsp	soy sauce	2 tsp
2 tbs	tomato purée (paste)	2 tbs
2 tbs	Mexican chili seasoning	2 tbs

1 Defrost the tofu. Drain thoroughly and squeeze the moisture out. Set aside.
2 Chop the onions. Sauté in the oil for 3–4 minutes over a fairly low heat until just tender.
3 Chop the carrot, celery and green (bell) pepper and add to the onions. Stir well and leave to cook for a further 2–3 minutes.
4 Chop the garlic and mushrooms finely. Add to the saucepan, stir, and cook for 4–5 minutes longer.
5 Chop the tomatoes. Add to the pan, along with the kidney beans, water, soy sauce, tomato purée (paste) and chili seasoning. Crumble the tofu into the saucepan. Stir well.
6 Cover the saucepan and leave to simmer over a very low heat for 10–15 minutes, stirring occasionally. Serve immediately.

Tofu chilli (chili) with macaroni

This dish is more like a casserole. Serve it with a green salad.

IMPERIAL/METRIC		AMERICAN
2	onions	2
2 sticks	celery	2 sticks
2	large green (bell) peppers	2
1 tbs	olive oil	1 tbs
2 × 14 oz (400g) tins	tomatoes	2 × 14–16 oz cans
2 tsp	Mexican chili seasoning	2 tsp
$^3/_4$–1 lb (340–455g)	firm tofu	$1^1/_2$–2 cups
2 tins (about 14 oz [400g] each)	kidney beans	28–32 oz cans (14–16 oz each)
$^1/_2$–$^3/_4$ lb (225–340g)	wholewheat macaroni	$^1/_2$–$^3/_4$ lb
as required	sea salt	as required

1 Chop the onions, celery and green (bell) peppers. Heat the oil in a pan and sauté the onions until tender. Add the celery and green (bell) peppers and sauté for a further 2–3 minutes.
2 Add the tomatoes and chili seasoning; bring to the boil. Crumble the tofu and add to the pan. Turn the heat down to low and simmer for 10–15 minutes. Add the kidney beans and simmer for a further 5 minutes.
3 Meanwhile, cook the macaroni in boiling salted water until just tender. Drain well.
4 Toss the macaroni with the tofu mixture, turn into an oiled casserole, and bake in the oven at 350°F (180°C, Gas Mark 4) for 30–40 minutes.

Tofu enchiladas

Undeniably a rather complicated and elaborate recipe, but the results justify the effort. Serve it with a green salad.

IMPERIAL/METRIC		AMERICAN
	Tortillas:	
5 oz (140g)	wholewheat flour	1¼ cups
3 oz (85g)	cornmeal	½ cup
pinch	sea salt	pinch
5 tbs	vegetable margarine	5 tbs
	Salsa:	
1	onion	1
2 cloves	garlic	2 cloves
2 tbs	vegetable oil	2 tbs
1 small tin (about 7 oz [200g])	tomatoes	1 can (about 7 oz)
2 tbs	Mexican chili seasoning	2 tbs
as required	freshly ground black pepper	as required
1 tsp	cumin seeds	1 tsp
¼ tsp	cayenne pepper	¼ tsp
5 oz (140g)	tomato purée (paste)	⅔ cup
¾ pint (425ml)	water	2 cups
	Filling:	
¾–1 lb (340–455g)	firm tofu	1½–2 cups
¼ pint (140ml)	soya (soy) yogurt	⅔ cup
as required	sea salt	as required
½ tsp	turmeric	½ tsp
¼ tsp	paprika	¼ tsp
2 oz (55g)	button mushrooms	1 cup
3–4	spring onions (scallions)	3–4
as required	black olives	as required

1   To make the tortillas, combine the flour and cornmeal in a bowl. Add a pinch of salt then blend in the margarine. Add enough water to form a dough. Make small balls out of the dough (the size does not matter, as you can make either

small or large tortillas), and roll them out with a rolling pin on a floured board. Place each tortilla on an ungreased frying pan over a moderately high heat. When it begins to bubble, turn it over until the other side begins to bubble. Remove from the heat, pile on a plate and set aside.

2   To make the salsa (sauce) chop the onion and garlic finely. Sauté in the oil until softened.

3   Chop the chillies (chilies) finely. Put the tomatoes and their juice into a liquidizer and blend thoroughly.

4   Add the chillies (chilies), chili seasoning, black pepper, cumin seeds, cayenne pepper, tomato purée (paste), blended tomatoes and water to the onion and garlic. Stir well. Bring to the boil, then simmer for about 20 minutes.

5   To make the filling mash the tofu and mix in the yogurt, salt, turmeric and paprika.

6   Chop the mushrooms and spring onions (scallions) finely and add to the tofu mixture. Chop the olives and set aside.

7   To assemble the dish, brush each tortilla with a little of the salsa, then spoon a little of the filling into the centre. Fold it over twice to form a rolled pancake shape. Cover the bottom of a baking sheet with a thin layer of salsa and place each filled tortilla on the sheet. When all the tortillas have been filled, spoon the remaining salsa over the top. If there is any filling left it can be used as decoration over the salsa. Finally, garnish with the chopped olives.

8   Bake the enchiladas in the oven at 350°F (180°C, Gas Mark 4) for about half an hour. Serve immediately.

Tofu, rice and courgette (zucchini) enchiladas

Another enchilada dish, which would be a good main course for a dinner party. Again, a green salad is the best accompaniment.

IMPERIAL/METRIC		AMERICAN
	Tortillas:	
5 oz (140g)	wholewheat flour	1¼ cups
3 oz (85g)	cornmeal	½ cup
pinch	sea salt	pinch
5 tbs	vegetable margarine	5 tbs
6 oz (170g)	brown rice	1 cup
1 tin (about 14 oz [400g])	tomatoes	1 can (14–16 oz)
to taste	Mexican chili seasoning	to taste
as required	chilli (chili) powder (optional)	as required
1	large onion	1
1 clove	garlic	1 clove
2 tbs	olive oil	2 tbs
2	courgettes (zucchini)	2
½–¾ lb (225–340g)	firm tofu	1–1½ cups
2 tbs	sesame seeds	2 tbs
2–3	spring onions (scallions)	2–3

1 Make the tortillas according to the instructions in the previous recipe.
2 Cook the rice in boiling salted water until tender and set aside. (This may be done in advance.)
3 Put the tomatoes into a liquidizer, add some chili seasoning and blend thoroughly. Taste, and if the flavour is not sufficiently strong stir in additional seasoning; if it is not spicy enough add a little chilli (chili) powder. (The main constituents of Mexican chili seasoning are cumin, oregano and chilli [chili] powder; a combination of these will produce a 'Mexican' flavour.)
4 Chop the onion and garlic. Sauté in the oil in a large saucepan until tender.

5   Chop the courgettes (zucchini) finely. Add to the onion and garlic, along with the rice. Crumble the tofu into this mixture, adding a little salt to taste. Mix thoroughly.
6   Dip each tortilla into the puréed tomatoes, then place on a baking sheet that has been oiled with olive oil and place a little filling on it. Roll up to close.
7   When all the tortillas have been filled spoon the remainder of the puréed tomatoes over the top and sprinkle with the sesame seeds. Bake in the oven at 375°F (190°C, Gas Mark 5) for about half an hour.
8   Chop the spring onions (scallions) finely and sprinkle over the enchiladas as garnish.

 # Burritos

Burritos are similar to enchiladas in being a type of savoury stuffed pancake, but they are made with wheat flour only. This is more of an everyday dish than the previous two recipes.

IMPERIAL/METRIC		AMERICAN
¾ lb (340g)	wholewheat flour	3 cups
1 tsp	sea salt	1 tsp
1 large	onion	1 large
4 oz (115g)	mushrooms	2 cups
2 tbs	vegetable oil	2 tbs
1 lb (455g)	firm tofu	2 cups
3 tsp	Mexican chili seasoning	3 tsp
2 tbs	soy sauce	2 tbs
1 tin (about 14 oz [400g])	tomatoes	1 can (14–16 oz)
2 tsp	ground cumin	2 tsp
½ tsp	dried basil	½ tsp
2 tsp	chopped parsley	2 tsp

1   Put the flour and salt in a large bowl and add enough water to make a dough. Cover with a damp cloth and leave for an hour or longer. Knead the dough,

then pull off individual lumps and roll each one out into a round on a floured board. Heat a heavy frying pan, and cook each round for a few minutes on each side before removing from the heat.

2   Chop the onion and mushrooms and sauté in the oil until tender. Crumble in the tofu and sprinkle with the chili seasoning. Cook for about 10 minutes longer, stirring frequently. Add the soy sauce.

3   Put the tomatoes into a liquidizer with the cumin, basil and parsley. Blend thoroughly.

4   Add half the blended tomatoes to the tofu mixture, and stir well. Fill the burritos with this mixture and roll up. Place on an oiled baking sheet and top with the rest of the tomato sauce. Bake in the oven at 350°F (180°C, Gas Mark 4) for 20–30 minutes.

 # Tofu rancheros

Traditionally this dish is made with scrambled eggs, but it works well with tofu. Serve with brown rice or tortillas.

IMPERIAL/METRIC		AMERICAN
1 tin (about 14 oz [400g])	tomatoes	1 can (14–16 oz)
1	onion	1
1	green (bell) pepper	1
1	red (bell) pepper	1
2 tbs	vegetable oil	2 tbs
2 tsp	Mexican chili seasoning	2 tsp
¹/₂ tsp	turmeric	¹/₂ tsp
1 oz (30g)	soya (soy) flour	¹/₄ cup
1 lb (455g)	firm tofu	2 cups

1   Drain the tomatoes (the juice will not be needed).

2   Chop the onion and peppers and sauté in the oil until just tender. Add the chili seasoning, turmeric, and soya (soy) flour. Stir well, then slowly add the tomatoes. Bring to the boil, lower the heat and simmer for about 5 minutes.

3 Put the tofu into a clean tea towel (dish towel) and squeeze well to extract the moisture.
4 Add the crumbled tofu to the tomato mixture. Heat for a minute or two before serving.

Tofu tacos

Taco shells are readily available both in Britain and the USA, and here is a quick and easy filling for them. This quantity is enough for a light lunch; for a full evening meal serve with Mexican rice and refried beans.

IMPERIAL/METRIC		AMERICAN
1	onion	1
2 cloves	garlic	2 cloves
3 tbs	vegetable oil	3 tbs
1 tbs	Mexican chili seasoning	1 tbs
2 tbs	wholewheat flour	2 tbs
1/2 pint (285ml)	water	1 1/3 cups
2 tbs	tomato purée (paste)	2 tbs
1 tsp	yeast extract	1 tsp
1/2 lb (225g)	firm tofu	1 cup
as required	sea salt	as required
as required	freshly ground black pepper	as required
1 packet (12)	taco shells	1 packet (12)
as required	lettuce	as required

1 Chop the onion and crush the garlic. Sauté in the oil for a few minutes until tender. Stir in the chili seasoning and the flour. Add the water slowly, stirring constantly until it comes to the boil. Stir in the tomato purée (paste) and the yeast extract.
2 Crumble the tofu into the sauce. Simmer, uncovered, for about 10 minutes or until thick. Taste and add salt and pepper if required.
3 Meanwhile, heat the tacos according to the instructions on the packet.
4 Fill the taco shells with the tofu mixture and top with shredded lettuce.

 # Tamale pie

Tamale pie is not a dish I have ever encountered in Britain, but it is popular in the USA. As with so many Mexican dishes, a green salad is the best accompaniment.

IMPERIAL/METRIC		AMERICAN
¹/₂ lb (225g)	cornmeal	1¹/₃ cups
as required	sea salt	as required
8 fl oz (225ml)	cold water	1 cup
³/₄ pint (425ml)	boiling water	2 cups
1	onion	1
2 tbs	vegetable oil	2 tbs
1 tin (about 14 oz [400g])	tomatoes	1 can (14–16 oz)
2 tbs	wholewheat flour	2 tbs
12	black olives	12
¹/₂ tsp	cayenne pepper	¹/₂ tsp
2 tsp	dried basil	2 tsp
6–8 oz (170–225g)	fresh, frozen or drained tinned (canned) sweetcorn (corn kernels)	1–1¹/₂ cups
¹/₂ lb (225g)	firm tofu	1 cup
2 tbs	vegetable margarine	2 tbs

1 Combine the cornmeal with a little salt and the cold water and boiling water.
2 Bring to the boil over direct heat, then place over a saucepan of boiling water, cover and leave to steam for about 15 minutes.
3 Chop the onion and sauté in the oil until tender.
4 Blend the tomatoes in a liquidizer.
5 Add the flour to the onion and stir well. Slowly stir in the blended tomatoes. Bring to the boil, stirring constantly.
6 Chop the olives finely. Add to the tomato sauce with the cayenne pepper, basil and sweetcorn (corn). Stir well.
7 Dice the tofu into small cubes and sauté in the margarine until golden brown.
8 Spoon the cornmeal mush into an ovenproof dish to cover the bottom and line the sides. Top with the tofu cubes. Pour the tomato sauce over the top.
9 Bake in the oven at 350°F (180°C, Gas Mark 4) for 45 minutes.

Central American-style smoky pasta and bean dish

Smoked tofu can also be used for dishes from this part of the world. Serve with a salad.

IMPERIAL/METRIC		AMERICAN
10 oz (285g)	wholewheat macaroni or other pasta shape	2½ cups
8–10 oz (225–285g)	smoked tofu	1–1¼ cups
4 cloves	garlic	4 cloves
2 tbs	vegetable oil	2 tbs
2 tins (about 14 oz [400g])	kidney beans	2 cans (14–16 oz each)
1 tbs	ground cumin	1 tbs
as required	freshly ground black pepper	as required
as required	sea salt	as required

1 Cook the pasta in salted boiling water until tender.
2 Meanwhile, dice the smoked tofu finely. Chop the garlic very finely. Fry in the oil in a frying pan over a medium heat until both the tofu and garlic are lightly browned.
3 Drain the kidney beans, retaining about 2 tbs of the liquid.
4 When the pasta is cooked drain it well. Put it back in the saucepan, along with the tofu and garlic, beans, bean liquid, cumin and black pepper (additional salt should not be necessary, but add a little sea salt if required). Mix well, then cook for a further 4–5 minutes over a very low heat before serving.

5

Mediterranean-style dishes

Tofu, mushroom and noodle casserole

This recipe uses tofu in two different ways. It is rich and creamy, an excellent dish for entertaining. Serve it with a fresh mixed salad.

IMPERIAL/METRIC		AMERICAN
10 oz (285g)	wholewheat noodles	2 cups
2	onions	2
4 tbs	vegetable oil	4 tbs
½ lb (225g)	mushrooms	4 cups
1–1¼ lb (455–565g)	firm tofu	2–2½ cups
3 tbs	wholewheat flour	3 tbs
1 tsp	dried basil	1 tsp
as required	sea salt	as required
as required	freshly ground black pepper	as required
2 tins (about 14 oz [400g] each)	tomatoes	2 cans (14–16 oz each)
juice of ½	lemon	juice of ½
2 tbs	tahini	2 tbs

1 Cook the noodles in salted boiling water until just tender.
2 Meanwhile, chop the onions and sauté in a large saucepan in 2 tbs of the oil for 2–3 minutes.
3 Slice the mushrooms, add them to the pan, and continue to cook until the onions and mushrooms are tender.
4 Dice half the tofu. Spread the flour out on a plate and mix in the basil and seasoning.
5 Roll the diced tofu in this mixture until well coated. Heat the remaining oil in a frying pan, and shallow-fry the diced tofu until golden, turning frequently.
6 Crumble the remaining tofu into a liquidizer or food processor. Add the tomatoes, lemon juice or tahini, and blend thoroughly.
7 Pour the tomato mixture into the saucepan containing the onion and

mushrooms, add the fried diced tofu and stir well. Finally, stir in the cooked, drained noodles. Add more seasoning if desired.

8 Transfer the mixture to an oiled casserole dish, and bake in the oven at 350°F (180°C, Gas Mark 4) for about 40 minutes.

 # Tofu risotto

Complete dishes like this one are always useful because there is no need to worry about vegetable accompaniments.

IMPERIAL/METRIC		AMERICAN
³/₄ lb (340g)	brown rice	2 cups
2 small	onions	2 small
3 oz (85g)	vegetable margarine	¹/₃ cup
as required	vegetable stock or water	as required
1 stick	celery	1 stick
1	green (bell) pepper	1
2 oz (55g)	mushrooms	1 cup
1 clove	garlic	1 clove
10–12 oz (285– 340g)	firm tofu	1¹/₄–1¹/₂ cups
2 tbs	cider vinegar or wine vinegar	2 tbs
2 oz (55g)	Smokey Snaps (soy bakon bits)	¹/₃ cup
¹/₂ tsp	dried basil	¹/₂ tsp
¹/₂ tsp	dried marjoram	¹/₂ tsp

1 Cover the rice with boiling water, leave to soak for several hours, then drain.

2 Chop 1 onion. Melt half the margarine in a pan and sauté the onion until tender. Add the rice, cover with vegetable stock or water, bring to the boil, then simmer.

3 Meanwhile, chop the remaining onion, the celery, green (bell) pepper and mushrooms. Crush the garlic and dice the tofu. Melt the remaining margarine in a separate pan and sauté the vegetables and tofu for a few minutes until tender. Add the vinegar, Smokey Snaps (soy bakon bits) and herbs. Cover and

simmer for about 5 minutes.

4   When the rice is nearly ready add the vegetable and tofu mixture to it, stirring well, and continue cooking until the liquid is completely absorbed.

Tofu cacciatore

This tofu and vegetable mixture is served on top of pasta, making it another complete meal.

IMPERIAL/METRIC		AMERICAN
1 small	onion	1 small
1	carrot	1
1 clove	garlic	1 clove
4 tbs	vegetable oil	4 tbs
1	bay leaf	1
5 oz (140g)	tomato purée (paste)	$^2/_3$ cup
$^2/_3$ pint (340ml)	water	$1^1/_2$ cups
$^1/_2$–$^3/_4$ lb (225–340g)	wholewheat macaroni or pasta shells	2–3 cups
1 lb (455g)	firm tofu	2 cups
1–2 oz (30–55g)	wholewheat flour	$^1/_4$–$^1/_2$ cup
1 tsp	dried basil	1 tsp
4 oz (115g)	fresh (shelled) or frozen peas	$^2/_3$ cup

1   Chop the onion, carrot and garlic, and sauté in half the oil, along with the bay leaf, for a few minutes. Add the tomato purée (paste) and water, bring to the boil and simmer for about 10 minutes.

2   Meanwhile, cook the macaroni or shells for 10–15 minutes in salted boiling water.

3   Cut the tofu into cubes. Dust lightly with the flour and basil and sauté in the remaining oil until lightly browned.

4   Add the tofu to the tomato sauce, along with the peas, and simmer until the peas are just tender.

5   Serve with the cooked macaroni or shells.

Tofu pizza

In Italy cheese is by no means considered an essential ingredient in a pizza: a well-flavoured tomato sauce is the key component. However, an all-vegetable topping means a low-protein dish, whereas by including tofu you get a new taste and texture plus protein.

IMPERIAL/METRIC		AMERICAN
	Dough:	
1 tsp	raw cane sugar	1 tsp
¹/₄ pint (140ml)	water at blood heat (a little more if required)	²/₃ cup
1 tsp	dried yeast	1 tsp
¹/₂ lb (225g)	wholewheat flour	2 cups
1 tsp	sea salt	1 tsp
	Topping:	
1	onion	1
2 cloves	garlic	2 cloves
2 tbs	olive oil	2 tbs
1 tin (about 14 oz [400g])	tomatoes	1 can (14–16 oz)
2 tbs	tomato purée (paste)	2 tbs
2 tsp	dried oregano	2 tsp
1 tsp	dried basil	1 tsp
as required	sea salt	as required
as required	freshly ground black pepper	as required
¹/₂–³/₄ lb (225–340g)	firm or medium tofu	1–1¹/₂ cups
2–4 oz (55–115g)	mushrooms	1–2 cups
1 small	green (bell) pepper	1 small
	Optional extras:	
as required	sliced olives, capers, onions, artichoke hearts	as required

1 Dissolve the sugar in half the water, then sprinkle in the yeast and mix with a fork. Cover and leave in a warm place for about 10 minutes, by which time it should be frothy. Put the flour and salt in a bowl, then pour in the yeast mixture, along with the remaining water. Add a little extra water if necessary

to make a moist dough. Knead for 5 minutes. Roll out the dough and use to line pizza pans. Cover and leave in a warm place for about half an hour.

2 Chop the onion and garlic and sauté in the olive oil until tender. Add the tomatoes, tomato purée (paste) and herbs, bring to the boil then simmer until thick – about half an hour. Season to taste.

3 Spread the sauce over the pizza base – you can make one large pizza or two small ones. (Any leftover sauce can be refrigerated for use within a week.) Crumble the tofu over the sauce.

4 Chop the mushrooms finely; thinly slice the green (bell) pepper. Arrange over the tofu along with any of the optional extras.

5 Bake in the oven at 450°F (230°C, Gas Mark 8) for about half an hour.

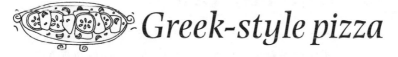 # Greek-style pizza

Italian pizzas always have a tomato base; here is a different – but no less delectable – type of pizza.

IMPERIAL/METRIC		AMERICAN
	Dough:	
1 tsp	raw cane sugar	1 tsp
¼ pint (140ml)	water at blood heat (a little more if required)	⅔ cup
1 tsp	dried yeast	1 tsp
½ lb (225g)	wholewheat flour	2 cups
1 tsp	sea salt	1 tsp
	Topping:	
1 large	onion	1 large
4 tbs	olive oil	4 tbs
¾ lb (340g)	fresh spinach	¾ lb
¾ lb (340g)	firm tofu	1½ cups
1 clove	garlic	1 clove
12	black olives	12
as required	sea salt	as required
as required	freshly ground black pepper	as required
1 tbs	dried oregano	1 tbs

1 Make the dough according to the instructions in the previous recipe.
2 Chop the onion and sauté in the oil until just tender.
3 Chop the spinach. Add to the onion and cover the pan for 3–4 minutes, until the spinach is limp.
4 Mash the tofu. Chop the garlic and olives finely. Add to the onion and spinach with salt and pepper to taste, and the oregano.
5 Bake the pizza crust in the oven at 400°F (200°C, Gas Mark 6) for about 5 minutes. Remove from the oven and top with the tofu/spinach mixture. Return to the oven and bake for 15–20 minutes until the crust is fully cooked.

 # Tofu calzone

A calzone is a folded-over, filled pizza. Traditionally it is made with a yeast dough as in the two recipes above, but a shortcrust pastry works well.

IMPERIAL/METRIC		AMERICAN
1	onion	1
1–2 cloves	garlic	1–2 cloves
2 tbs	olive oil	2 tbs
1	carrot	1
2 sticks	celery	2 sticks
1 small	green (bell) pepper	1 small
2 oz (55g)	mushrooms	1 cup
4 tbs	tomato purée (paste)	4 tbs
3 fl oz (90ml)	water	1/3 cup
1 tsp	dried basil	1 tsp
1 tsp	dried oregano	1 tsp
1/2 lb (225g)	firm or medium tofu	1 cup
1/2 lb (225g)	wholewheat flour	2 cups
as required	sea salt	as required
4 oz (115g)	vegetable margarine	1/2 cup

1 Chop the onion and garlic and sauté in the olive oil for 3–4 minutes.
2 Chop the carrot, celery and green (bell) pepper and add to the pan. Chop the mushrooms and add to the pan when the other vegetables are nearly tender. Stir in the tomato purée (paste), water, basil and oregano and bring to the boil. Cut the tofu into cubes and add to the pan. Lower the heat and simmer for 5 minutes. Cool slightly.
3 Put the flour and salt in a bowl and mix in the margarine. Add enough water to make a dough, divide into 4 pieces, and roll out into circles on a floured board.
4 Spoon a quarter of the filling on to a half of each circle. Fold the dough over to cover, and pinch it well to seal.
5 Bake in the oven at 375°F (190°C, Gas Mark 5) for 25–35 minutes until the crust is browned.

Aubergine (Eggplant) tofuiana

Eggplant parmigiana is a popular Italian dish in the USA. Here is my version using tofu. Serve it on its own or with salad for a light lunch, or with potatoes or rice for a more substantial meal.

IMPERIAL/METRIC		AMERICAN
1 tin (about 14 oz [400g])	tomatoes	1 can (14–16 oz)
1	onion	1
2 cloves	garlic	2 cloves
3 tsp	dried basil	3 tsp
1 tbs plus additional as required	vegetable oil	1 tbs plus additional as required
1–1½ lb (455–680g)	aubergines (eggplants)	1–1½ lb
as required	fine breadcrumbs or wholewheat flour	as required
³/₄–1 lb (340–455g)	firm tofu	1½–2 cups

1　Blend the tomatoes in a liquidizer then pour into a saucepan. Chop the onion and crush the garlic, add to the saucepan along with the basil and the 1 tbs vegetable oil. Stir well, bring to the boil, then lower the heat and simmer for about 20 minutes.
2　Slice the aubergines (eggplants) very thinly. Brush each slice with a little oil on both sides, then dip into fine breadcrumbs or flour. Put the slices under the grill (broiler) and grill (broil) until tender, turning them over once. (Alternatively, shallow-fry the slices in a little oil and drain well.)
3　Arrange half the aubergine (eggplant) slices in an oiled baking dish, crumble half the tofu over them, top with half the tomato sauce. Repeat the layers.
4　Bake in the oven at 350°F (180°C, Gas Mark 4) for 20–30 minutes.

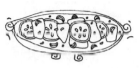 # Tagliatelle with creamy tofu sauce

This is amazingly quick and easy, and if you use a quarter of the ingredients it is ideal for one person. A crisp green salad would provide a good contrast of texture and flavour.

IMPERIAL/METRIC		AMERICAN
3/4 lb (340g)	medium tofu	1 1/2 cups
1/4 pint (140ml)	soya (soy) yogurt	2/3 cup
1 tbs	tahini	1 tbs
2 heaped tsp	miso	2 heaped tsp
1 tbs	lemon juice	1 tbs
12–14 oz (340–400g)	wholewheat tagliatelle	2 1/2 cups
as required	freshly ground black pepper	as required

1 Put the tofu, yogurt, tahini, miso and lemon juice in a liquidizer and blend well.
2 Cook the pasta in salted boiling water until just tender and drain.
3 Toss the tagliatelle with the tofu sauce, grind some black pepper over the top and serve at once.

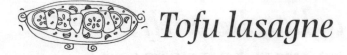 # *Tofu lasagne*

In the USA one can buy a frozen version of this dish at health-food stores, but there is nothing like a homemade lasagne. Serve with a green salad.

IMPERIAL/METRIC		AMERICAN
1 large	onion	1 large
1 clove	garlic	1 clove
2 tins (about 14 oz [400g] each)	tomatoes	2 cans (14–16 oz each)
1 tbs	dried basil	1 tbs
2 tsp	raw cane sugar	2 tsp
as required	sea salt	as required
as required	freshly ground black pepper	as required
8–10 oz (225g–285g)	wholewheat lasagne	8–10 oz
12–14 oz (340–400g)	medium or firm tofu	$1^1/_2$–$1^3/_4$ cups

1 Chop the onion and garlic finely. Combine the tomatoes in a saucepan with the onion, garlic, basil, sugar and seasoning. Cook for about half an hour until thickened.
2 Cook the lasagne in salted boiling water until tender (15–20 minutes). Drain well.
3 Mash the tofu.
4 Place alternate layers of lasagne, tofu and tomato sauce in an ovenproof dish, starting with lasagne and ending with tomato sauce.
5 Bake in the oven at 375°F (190°C, Gas Mark 5) for 45 minutes.

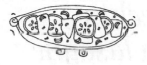

Spinach and mushroom lasagne

This dish would be a good choice for entertaining dinner guests.

IMPERIAL/METRIC		AMERICAN
1 lb (455g)	spinach	1 lb
2 oz (55g)	vegetable margarine	1/4 cup
1 tsp	dried marjoram	1 tsp
as required	sea salt	as required
as required	freshly ground black pepper	as required
3/4–1 lb (340–455g)	firm tofu	1 1/2–2 cups
1/2 lb (225g)	mushrooms	4 cups
4 tbs	wholewheat flour	4 tbs
2 tsp	soy sauce	2 tsp
8–10 oz (225–285g)	wholewheat lasagne	8–10 oz

1 Wash the spinach well, then cook it in a saucepan without additional water until it is just tender. Drain, reserving the liquid.
2 Chop the spinach coarsely, and while it is still warm mix in half the margarine. Season with the marjoram, salt and pepper, then crumble the tofu into the spinach mixture and combine thoroughly.
3 Chop the mushrooms finely. Sauté in the remaining margarine until tender. Stir in the flour. Make up the spinach liquid with water to 1 pint (285ml, 1 1/3 cups) and stir it into the mushrooms gradually until it thickens and boils. Mix in the soy sauce.
4 Cook the lasagne in salted boiling water until tender (15–20 minutes). Drain well.
5 Place alternate layers of lasagne, spinach/tofu mixture, and mushroom sauce in an ovenproof dish, finishing with mushroom sauce.
6 Bake in the oven at 400°F (200°C, Gas Mark 6) for half an hour.

Courgette (Zucchini) and mushroom lasagne with tofu topping

Yet another version of lasagne. This too would be a good dinner party dish, served with a colourful mixed salad.

IMPERIAL/METRIC		AMERICAN
8–10 oz (225–285g)	wholewheat lasagne	8–10 oz
2	onions	2
2 tbs	olive oil	2 tbs
2 cloves	garlic	2 cloves
$^{1}/_{2}$–$^{3}/_{4}$ lb (225–340g)	mushrooms	4–6 cups
$^{1}/_{2}$–$^{3}/_{4}$ lb (225–340g)	courgettes (zucchini)	$^{1}/_{2}$–$^{3}/_{4}$ lb
$^{3}/_{4}$ lb (340g)	tomatoes	$^{3}/_{4}$ lb
1 tbs	tomato purée (paste)	1 tbs
2 tsp	dried oregano	2 tsp
1 tsp	dried basil	1 tsp
as required	sea salt	as required
as required	freshly ground black pepper	as required
$1^{1}/_{4}$–$1^{1}/_{2}$ lb (565–680g)	medium tofu	$2^{1}/_{2}$–3 cups
3 tbs	tahini	3 tbs
juice of 1	lemon	juice of 1
4 tbs	soya (soy) yogurt	4 tbs

1   Cook the lasagne in salted boiling water until tender, drain and rinse.
2   Chop the onions and sauté in the oil for 3–4 minutes. Crush the garlic and add to the pan; cook for a couple of minutes longer.
3   Chop the mushrooms and courgettes (zucchini) and add to the onions and garlic. Cook for 2–3 minutes.

4   Cover the tomatoes with boiling water for 1 minute, drain, peel and chop them. Add to the vegetables with the tomato purée (paste) and the herbs. Cover the pan and cook for 5–10 minutes. Season to taste.

5   Put the tofu, tahini, lemon juice and yogurt into a liquidizer and blend thoroughly. Stir in salt and pepper to taste.

6   Layer the lasagne and vegetables in a baking dish. Pour the tofu mixture over the top. Bake in the oven at 350°F (180°C, Gas Mark 4) for 35–40 minutes, when it should be nicely browned on top.

 # *Tofu ravioli*

For a quick and easy tomato sauce to serve with this dish follow the recipe for the one in Aubergine (Eggplant) tofuiana (page 80); otherwise use one of the natural tomato sauces available at health-food stores.

IMPERIAL/METRIC		AMERICAN
³/₄ lb (340g)	wholemeal flour (or 84% flour)	3 cups
2 tbs	soya (soy) flour	2 tbs
pinch	sea salt	pinch
¹/₄ pint (140ml)	warm water	²/₃ cup
¹/₂ lb (225g)	firm tofu	1 cup
¹/₂ tsp	onion salt	¹/₂ tsp
¹/₂ tsp	garlic salt	¹/₂ tsp
as required	freshly ground black pepper	as required

1   Mix the flour, soya (soy) flour and salt together in a bowl and add the water to make a dough (do this slowly as different flours require slightly different quantites of liquid, and once the consistency of a dough has been reached no more water should be added). Knead well and set aside.

2   Mash the tofu in a mixing bowl. Stir in the onion and garlic salts and a little black pepper.

3   Divide the dough into 4 or more sections and roll out on a floured board. Cut out small squares. Place a little filling on to a square, cover with

another square, and seal all round the edges with a fork to secure the filling inside.

4 Drop the squares into a large pan of salted boiling water and cook for 10 minutes. Drain well, and serve with tomato sauce.

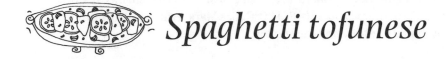 # Spaghetti tofunese

Who needs Bolognese when you can have tofunese?

IMPERIAL/METRIC		AMERICAN
1 large	onion	1 large
2	carrots	2
2 sticks	celery	2 sticks
4 oz (115g)	mushrooms	2 cups
3 tbs	vegetable oil	3 tbs
1 tin (about 14 oz [400g])	tomatoes	1 can (14–16 oz)
8–10 oz (225–285g)	firm tofu	1–1¼ cups
2 tsp	yeast extract	2 tsp
1 tsp	chilli (chili) powder (optional)	1 tsp
2 tbs	chopped parsley	2 tbs
2 tsp	dried basil	2 tsp
³/₄ lb (340g)	wholewheat spaghetti	³/₄ lb

1 Chop the onion, carrots, celery and mushrooms. Sauté in the oil for a few minutes.

2 Add the tomatoes and bring to the boil. Crumble the tofu into the pan. Stir in the yeast extract, chilli (chili) powder (if used), parsley and basil.

3 Simmer the mixture for about 20 minutes, uncovered. Meanwhile cook the spaghetti in salted boiling water until tender. Drain and serve with the sauce.

Spaghetti with tofu and peas

Another spaghetti dish, a really quick and easy one. For one person use a quarter of the ingredients.

IMPERIAL/METRIC		AMERICAN
³/₄ lb (340g)	wholewheat spaghetti	³/₄ lb
¹/₂ lb (225g)	fresh (shelled) or frozen peas	1¹/₃ cups
3 cloves	garlic	3 cloves
2 tbs	olive oil	2 tbs
2 tbs	vegetable margarine	2 tbs
1 lb (425g)	medium or firm tofu	2 cups
2 tbs	soy sauce	2 tbs
3 tbs	chopped parsley	3 tbs
as required	freshly ground black pepper	as required

1   Cook the spaghetti in salted boiling water until tender.
2   Meanwhile, cook the peas in salted boiling water in a separate pan until just tender. Drain. Crush the garlic. Heat the oil and margarine in a pan and add the garlic. Cook for 1–2 minutes until the garlic has turned light brown. Mash the tofu and add to the saucepan, along with the soy sauce. Heat gently.
3   Add the cooked peas and the parsley to the tofu mixture and heat for 1–2 minutes. Serve the tofu mixture over the spaghetti. Grind black pepper over the top before serving.

 # Persian carrots and nuts with saffron pilav

This dish doesn't need any accompaniments.

IMPERIAL/METRIC		AMERICAN
³/₄ lb (340g)	brown rice	2 cups
¹/₄ tsp	saffron threads	¹/₄ tsp
4	cardamom pods	4
2	onions	2
3 oz (85g)	vegetable margarine	¹/₃ cup
3 × 1 inch (2.5cm) pieces	cinnamon stick	3 × 1 inch pieces
4	cloves	4
as required	sea salt	as required
¹/₂–³/₄ lb (225–340g)	carrots	¹/₂–³/₄ lb
5	dates	5
1 tbs	raisins	1 tbs
1 tbs	cider vinegar or wine vinegar	1 tbs
2 tbs	lemon juice	2 tbs
¹/₂–³/₄ lb (225–340g)	medium or firm tofu	1–1¹/₂ cups
¹/₂ tsp	turmeric	¹/₂ tsp
as required	freshly ground black pepper	as required
2 tbs	blanched flaked (slivered) almonds	2 tbs

1 Cover the rice with boiling water, leave to soak for several hours, then drain.
2 Crush the saffron threads and soak in a little hot water for about 15 minutes.
3 To make the pilav, remove the seeds from the cardamom pods and chop 1 onion. Melt 2 oz (55g, ¹/₄ cup) of the margarine in a pan and add the cardamom seeds, cinnamon and cloves. Fry, stirring constantly, for 2 minutes. Add the chopped onion and fry, stirring occasionally, for several minutes, until golden brown.

4 Add the rice and cook over a low heat for 3–4 minutes. Cover with water, add the salt and the saffron water; bring to the boil, then lower the heat and simmer for about 15–20 minutes until the rice is tender and the liquid absorbed.
5 Meanwhile, peel the carrots and thinly slice them crossways. Melt the remaining margarine in a pan, add the carrots and sauté for a few minutes, stirring frequently.
6 Chop the remaining onion. Add to the carrots and sauté until soft.
7 Chop the dates. Add to the carrot mixture with the raisins, vinegar and lemon juice. Cover the saucepan, lower the heat, and simmer for about 15–20 minutes.
8 Meanwhile, mash the tofu in a bowl with the turmeric, black pepper and a little salt.
9 When the carrots are tender, add the mashed tofu and stir well until the tofu is thoroughly heated.
10 Serve on the saffron pilav, sprinkled with the almonds.

Spanish nomlette

Spanish omelettes have potatoes and other vegetables mixed into them. Here is a cholesterol-free version. A nice, light luncheon dish.

IMPERIAL/METRIC		AMERICAN
³/₄ lb (340g)	potatoes	³/₄ lb
2	tomatoes	2
2	tinned (canned) pimentos	2
2 small	onions	2 small
3 tbs	olive oil	3 tbs
4 tbs	cooked peas	4 tbs
1¹/₂ lbs (680g)	firm or medium tofu	3 cups
2 oz (55g)	wholewheat flour	¹/₂ cup
1¹/₂ tsp	baking powder	1¹/₂ tsp
as required	sea salt	as required
as required	freshly ground black pepper	as required

1 Cook the potatoes in salted boiling water. Drain then dice them. Peel and chop the tomatoes. Chop the pimentos.

2 Chop the onions. Sauté in the oil for 2–3 minutes, then add the tomatoes, pimentos, potatoes and peas. Fry for a few minutes, stirring.

3 Put 4 oz (115g, ¹/₂ cup) of the tofu into a liquidizer and blend until creamy (if necessary add a little water).

4 Mash the remaining tofu in a large mixing bowl. Add the blended tofu, the flour and the baking powder, and mix well.

5 Add the vegetable mixture to the tofu mixture, and mix well, adding seasoning.

6 Form the mixture into 4 patties and place on an oiled baking sheet. Bake in the oven for about half an hour at 325°F (170°C, Gas Mark 3) then flip the patties over and cook for a further 15 minutes.

 # Spanish tofu spaghetti

For a really quick and easy dish this one would be hard to beat. And it is simple to make for one person; just use a quarter of the ingredients.

IMPERIAL/METRIC		AMERICAN
³/₄ lb (340g)	wholewheat spaghetti	³/₄ lb
2	onions	2
2	green (bell) peppers	2
3 tbs	olive oil	3 tbs
³/₄–1 lb (340–455g)	firm or medium tofu	1¹/₂–2 cups
2 tsp	turmeric	2 tsp
2 tsp	garlic salt	2 tsp
as required	freshly ground black pepper	as required

1 Cook the spaghetti in salted boiling water until just tender. Drain and set aside.
2 Chop the onions and green (bell) peppers. Sauté in the olive oil in a frying pan until tender and lightly browned.
3 Mash the tofu. Add the turmeric, garlic salt, and black pepper to taste, and mix well.
4 Add the tofu to the frying pan and stir until thoroughly heated.
5 Stir in the cooked spaghetti and fry for a few minutes longer before serving.

Arroz con tofu

In the USA there is a dish called 'Spanish rice' which bears no resemblance to anything you would find in Spain. Tofu may not be an authentic Spanish ingredient, but if a Spaniard tasted this he or she would feel at home.

IMPERIAL/METRIC		AMERICAN
¾ lb (340g)	brown rice	2 cups
1 large	onion	1 large
1 large or 2 small	green (bell) peppers	1 large or 2 small
2 cloves	garlic	2 cloves
4 tbs	olive oil	4 tbs
1 tin (about 14 oz [400g])	tomatoes	1 can (14–16 oz)
½ pint (285 ml)	vegetable stock or water	1⅓ cups
½ tsp	saffron	½ tsp
as required	sea salt	as required
as required	freshly ground black pepper	as required
1 lb (455g)	firm tofu	2 cups
1 oz (30g)	vegetable margarine	2 tbs
1 small tin (about 7 oz [200g])	pimentos	1 can (7½ oz)
4 oz (115g)	fresh (shelled) or frozen peas	⅔ cup

1 Cover the rice with boiling water and leave to soak for several hours.
2 Chop the onion and green (bell) peppers; crush the garlic. Sauté in the olive oil in a saucepan until just tender.
3 Drain the rice and add to the pan, with the tomatoes and stock or water. Bring to the boil, then stir in the saffron and seasoning. Lower the heat and simmer.
4 Cut the tofu into cubes. Sauté in the margarine until golden. Add to the rice mixture and stir well.
5 Chop the pimentos. When the rice is tender and the liquid nearly absorbed (15–20 minutes), add the pimentos and peas. Cook for a further 3–4 minutes before serving.

Courgette (Zucchini) mushroom and rice savoury

A self-contained dish which could be served with a salad if desired, or with potatoes for a really filling meal.

IMPERIAL/METRIC		AMERICAN
½ lb (225g)	brown rice	1⅓ cups
1	onion	1
1 clove	garlic	1 clove
3 tbs	vegetable margarine	3 tbs
¾ lb (340g)	courgettes (zucchini)	¾ lb
¾ lb (340g)	mushrooms	6 cups
2 tsp	dried oregano	2 tsp
1 tsp	dried basil	1 tsp
1¼ lb (565g)	medium or firm tofu	2½ cups
4 tbs	nutritional yeast	4 tbs
as required	sea salt	as required
as required	freshly ground black pepper	as required

1 Cook the rice in salted boiling water until tender. (This may be done in advance if desired.)
2 Chop the onion. Crush the garlic. Melt the margarine in a frying pan and sauté the onion and garlic for 3–4 minutes.
3 Halve or quarter the courgettes (zucchini) lengthwise, depending on size, then slice them fairly thinly. Chop the mushrooms coarsely. Add the courgettes (zucchini) and mushrooms to the frying pan, along with the oregano and basil, and sauté for 4–5 minutes.
4 Mash the tofu and mix together with the rice. Stir in the vegetables and half the yeast; season to taste. Turn into a greased casserole, sprinkle the remaining yeast on top, and bake in the oven at 375°F (190°C, Gas Mark 5) for 25–30 minutes until nicely set.

 *Risi e bisi*

Smoked tofu can add a new dimension to Italian dishes. For a single serving of this one use a quarter of the ingredients.

IMPERIAL/METRIC		AMERICAN
³/₄ lb (340g)	brown rice	2 cups
2 tsp	yeast extract	2 tsp
6 oz (170g)	smoked tofu	³/₄ cup
2 tbs	vegetable margarine	2 tbs
2 tbs	olive oil	2 tbs
1 oz (30g)	chopped parsley	1 cup
2 sticks	celery	2 sticks
1 lb (455g)	fresh (shelled) or frozen peas	1 lb
4 tbs	cider vinegar or wine vinegar	4 tbs
as required	sea salt	as required
as required	freshly ground black pepper	as required
3 tbs	nutritional yeast	3 tbs

1 Put the rice in a pan, cover with boiling water, and add the yeast extract instead of salt. Cook until the rice is tender and the water is absorbed.
2 Cut the smoked tofu into small cubes. Sauté the cubes in the margarine and olive oil for about 5 minutes.
3 Chop the parsley and celery, add them to the smoked tofu, and cook for a further 3–4 minutes. Add the peas and vinegar, stir well, raise the heat for 2–3 minutes, then cover the saucepan, lower the heat and cook for a few minutes until just tender.
4 Stir this mixture into the cooked rice and leave for 1–2 minutes longer. Finally, stir in the seasoning and the yeast. Serve immediately.

 # *Spaghetti Milanese*

Another complete dish utilizing smoked tofu, and another one easy to make for a single person by using a quarter of the ingredients.

IMPERIAL/METRIC		AMERICAN
³/₄ lb (340g)	wholewheat spaghetti	³/₄ lb
1	onion	1
4 oz (115g)	mushrooms	2 cups
3 tbs	vegetable margarine	3 tbs
grating	nutmeg	grating
pinch	dried thyme	pinch
as required	freshly ground black pepper	as required
1 tin (about 14 oz [400g])	tomatoes	1 can (14–16 oz)
¹/₂ lb (225g)	smoked tofu	1 cup
as required	nutritional yeast	as required

1 Cook the spaghetti in salted boiling water until tender.
2 Meanwhile, chop the onion and mushrooms and cook in 2 tbs of the margarine for 3–5 minutes.
3 Add the nutmeg, thyme, black pepper and tomatoes and stir well. Bring to the boil, lower the heat and simmer for about 15 minutes.
4 Chop the smoked tofu into small dice and add to the saucepan. Cook for a further 5 minutes.
5 Drain the spaghetti and toss with the remaining margarine.
6 Serve the spaghetti with the sauce poured over it, sprinkled with yeast.

Bean and smoked tofu Napoli

A double helping of protein, with both beans and smoked tofu. Serve with rice or pasta.

IMPERIAL/METRIC		AMERICAN
2	onions	2
2 tbs	olive oil	2 tbs
2–3 cloves	garlic	2–3 cloves
3 sticks	celery	3 sticks
2 tins (about 14 oz [400g] each)	chopped tomatoes	2 cans (14–16 oz each)
¹/₂ lb (225g)	smoked tofu	1 cup
2 tins (about 14 oz [400g] each)	haricot (navy) beans	2 cans (14–16 oz each)
3 tbs	tomato purée (paste)	3 tbs
1 tbs	dried basil	1 tbs
as required	freshly ground black pepper	as required
2 tbs	chopped parsley	2 tbs

1 Chop the onions. Heat the oil in a large saucepan and sauté the chopped onions for 2–3 minutes. Crush the garlic and stir it in; sauté for another 1–2 minutes.

2 Chop the celery finely and add to the pan along with the tomatoes. Bring to the boil. Meanwhile, drain and dice the smoked tofu and add it to the pan. Stir well, cook for 2–3 minutes, then add the tomato purée (paste), basil and some freshly ground black pepper. Lower the heat, cover the pan, and leave to simmer for 15–20 minutes. Drain and add the beans, and heat through. Garnish with the parsley.

6
Indian-style Dishes

Curried tofu

The blandness of tofu allows it to absorb the myriad flavours of Indian spices. This dish is fragrant, not 'hot'. Serve it with rice.

IMPERIAL/METRIC		AMERICAN
2	onions	2
1 clove	garlic	1 clove
2 oz (55g)	vegetable margarine	1/4 cup
2 tsp	coriander seeds	2 tsp
2 tsp	black peppercorns	2 tsp
1 tsp	cumin seeds	1 tsp
1 tsp	cardamom pods	1 tsp
1/4 inch (0.75cm) piece	cinnamon stick	1/4 inch piece
1 tsp	ground cloves	1 tsp
2 tsp	turmeric	2 tsp
2 tsp	wholewheat flour	2 tsp
1–1 1/2 lb (455–680g)	firm tofu	2–3 cups
1/2 pint (285ml)	vegetable stock	1 1/3 cups
1 tsp	raw cane sugar	1 tsp
as required	sea salt	as required
juice of 1/2	lemon	juice of 1/2

1   Chop the onions and finely chop the garlic. Melt the margarine in a pan and sauté the onions and garlic until just tender.
2   Grind the coriander seeds, peppercorns and cumin seeds; peel the cardamom pods and grind the seeds with a mortar and pestle. Add all the spices, including the cinnamon stick, cloves and turmeric, to the onions and garlic, along with the flour, and stir well.
3   Cut the tofu into cubes and add it to the pan. Stir well to coat thoroughly with the spices. Add the vegetable stock and bring to the boil. Simmer for 10 minutes.
4   Add the sugar and salt and simmer for a further 10 minutes. Finally, add the lemon juice just before serving.

Tofu pilau

This is a simple, self-contained dish.

IMPERIAL/METRIC		AMERICAN
³/₄ lb (340g)	brown rice	2 cups
2	onions	2
2 oz (55g)	vegetable margarine	¹/₄ cup
2	bay leaves	2
as required	sea salt	as required
³/₄–1 lb (340–455g)	firm tofu	1¹/₂–2 cups
2 tsp	turmeric	2 tsp
¹/₂ tsp	chilli (chili) powder	¹/₂ tsp
2 tsp	garam masala	2 tsp
2 tsp	lemon juice	2 tsp
2	tomatoes	2

1 Cover the rice with boiling water and leave to soak for several hours. Drain well.

2 Chop the onions and sauté in half the margarine for 3–4 minutes. Add the rice, bay leaves and salt; cover with boiling water and simmer until nearly tender (about 15 minutes).

3 Cut the tofu into cubes. Melt the remaining margarine in a separate pan and add the turmeric, chilli (chili) powder and garam masala; fry for 2–3 minutes then add the lemon juice. Stir the tofu cubes into the pan and leave to cook gently for 3–4 minutes before removing from the heat.

4 Add the tofu mixture to the nearly done rice and stir well. Continue simmering until the rice is tender and the water absorbed.

5 Before serving, remove the bay leaves and garnish with sliced tomatoes.

Saag (Spinach) tofu

Paneer is an Indian dairy cheese used in many traditional recipes. Tofu has a very similar texture and can be used in its place to make such dishes dairy-free. Serve with plain brown rice, pilau rice, or with an Indian bread.

IMPERIAL/METRIC		AMERICAN
$^1/_2$–$^3/_4$ lb (225–340g)	firm or medium tofu	1–1$^1/_2$ cups
3 tbs plus additional for deep-frying	vegetable oil	3 tbs plus additional for deep-frying
1 tsp	garam masala	1 tsp
1 tsp	sea salt	1 tsp
about 1 inch (2.5cm) piece	fresh ginger	about 1 inch piece
3 cloves	garlic	3 cloves
1	fresh green chilli (chili)	1
1–1$^1/_2$ lb (455g–680g)	spinach	1–1$^1/_2$ lb
4 tbs	soya (soy) milk	4 tbs

1 Cut the tofu into cubes and deep-fry in the oil until golden brown. Drain. While still hot sprinkle with the garam masala and half the salt. Set aside.
2 Peel the ginger, chop it and the garlic and chilli (chili) and put into a liquidizer or food processor with 4 tablespoons water. Blend until smooth.
3 Wash and coarsely chop the spinach.
4 Heat the 3 tbs vegetable oil in a saucepan, and add the ginger-garlic-chilli (chili) paste. Stir for about 30 seconds, then add the spinach and the remaining salt. Stir for a minute, then cover the saucepan and leave to simmer for 5–10 minutes (there should be enough water clinging to the spinach leaves to cook them, but if necessary add 1–2 tbs water).
5 Add the tofu cubes and milk to the pan, stir gently, and leave to simmer for a further 5–10 minutes, stirring once or twice.

Scrambled tofu with spicy tomato topping

A pleasant light lunch with an exotic flavour. For a single serving use a quarter of the ingredients (and perhaps a pinch of chilli [chili] powder instead of fresh chilli [chili]).

IMPERIAL/METRIC		AMERICAN
1 lb (455g)	firm tofu	1 lb
4	spring onions (scallions)	4
1	fresh green chilli (chili)	1
2 cloves	garlic	2 cloves
about ¼ inch (0.75cm) piece	fresh ginger	about ¼ inch piece
2 tbs	coriander seeds	2 tbs
3 tbs	vegetable oil	3 tbs
1½ tsp	black mustard seeds	1½ tsp
½ tsp	sea salt	½ tsp
1–1½ lb (455–680g)	firm or medium tofu	2–3 cups
4 tsp	turmeric	4 tsp
2 tbs	soy sauce	2 tbs
1 oz (30g)	vegetable margarine	2 tbs
8–12 slices	wholewheat toast	8–12 slices

1 Peel and chop the tomatoes. Chop the spring onions (scallions), chilli (chili) and garlic finely; peel and grate the ginger finely. Grind the coriander seeds.
2 Heat the oil in a saucepan. When hot, put in the mustard seeds. After a few seconds, when they have begun to pop, add the spring onions (scallions) and garlic. Stir for about 3 minutes, then add the tomatoes, ginger, coriander, and chilli (chili). Stir and cook over a medium heat for 6–8 minutes, then add the salt.
3 Meanwhile, mash the tofu in a bowl. Mix in the turmeric and soy sauce. Heat the margarine in a frying pan, and fry the tofu in it, stirring and turning it over frequently, for about 5 minutes.
4 Serve the scrambled tofu on the toast, topped with the tomato mixture.

 # Rice with tofu and peas

A self-contained dish based on a traditional paneer *(Indian cheese) recipe.*

IMPERIAL/METRIC		AMERICAN
³/₄ lb (340g)	brown rice	2 cups
1	fresh green chilli (chili)	1
4 tbs plus additional for deep-frying	vegetable oil	4 tbs plus additional for deep-frying
2	bay leaves	2
1 inch (2.5cm) piece	cinnamon stick	1 inch piece
5	cardamom pods	5
1 tsp	ground cumin	1 tsp
as required	sea salt	as required
¹/₂–³/₄ lb (225–340g)	medium or firm tofu	1–1¹/₂ cups
¹/₂ lb (225g)	fresh (shelled) or frozen peas	1¹/₃ cups

1   Cover the rice with boiling water, leave to soak for several hours then drain.
2   Chop the chilli (chili) finely.
3   Heat the 4 tbs vegetable oil in a pan and add the bay leaves, cinnamon, cardamom pods, cumin and chilli (chili). Stir once, then add the rice, stirring over a medium heat for 3–5 minutes. Cover with water and add a little salt; bring to the boil, then cover and simmer.
4   Meanwhile, cut the tofu into small cubes and deep-fry in the oil until golden brown.
5   When the rice is very nearly ready, add the peas, and cook until just tender. Add the tofu cubes and stir well so that they are thoroughly heated before serving.

Spaghetti Madras

Unlike most of the recipes in this chapter, this one makes no claim to authenticity; one would not find such a dish in Madras. Still, it's unusual and tasty, which is what really matters.

IMPERIAL/METRIC		AMERICAN
¹/₂ lb (225g)	medium or firm tofu	1 cup
as required	vegetable oil for deep-frying	as required
1	onion	1
2 oz (55g)	vegetable margarine	¹/₄ cup
³/₄ lb (340g)	cabbage	³/₄ lb
2–3	tomatoes	2–3
1 tsp	turmeric	1 tsp
¹/₄ tsp	mustard powder	¹/₄ tsp
pinch	cayenne pepper	pinch
1 tin (about 5 oz [140g])	tomato purée (paste)	1 can (5 oz)
¹/₄ pint (140ml)	water	²/₃ cup
¹/₂ lb (225g)	wholewheat spaghetti	¹/₂ lb
1 oz (30g)	seedless raisins	¹/₆ cup

1 Cut the tofu into cubes and deep-fry in the oil until golden. Drain and set aside.
2 Chop the onion and sauté in half the margarine until just tender. Shred the cabbage; skin and chop the tomatoes. Add to the onions along with the turmeric, mustard powder and cayenne pepper. Combine the tomato purée (paste) and water and add to the vegetables, along with the deep-fried tofu cubes. Cook, covered, for about 10 minutes.
3 Meanwhile, cook the spaghetti in salted boiling water until tender. Blanch the raisins in a little boiling water. Drain the spaghetti and toss with the remaining margarine.
4 Pour the sauce over the spaghetti and sprinkle with the raisins.

Tofu patia with vermicelli

Patia is a dish found on the menus of many Indian restaurants – though not, hitherto, with tofu as one of the ingredients. Traditionally it is served with rice, but vermicelli makes a pleasing change.

IMPERIAL/METRIC		AMERICAN
2	onions	2
1	green (bell) pepper	1
4 tbs	vegetable oil	4 tbs
3 cloves	garlic	3 cloves
2	fresh green chillies (chilies)	2
1 tsp	finely chopped fresh ginger	1 tsp
1 tsp	ground cumin	1 tsp
1 lb (455g)	firm tofu	2 cups
4 tsp	turmeric	4 tsp
1 tin (about 14 oz [400g])	tomatoes	1 can (14–16 oz)
4 tbs	water	4 tbs
as required	sea salt	as required
³/₄ lb (340g)	vermicelli	³/₄ lb

1   Slice the onions thinly. Chop the green pepper finely.
2   Heat the oil in a heavy frying pan. Sauté the onions and green (bell) pepper for 3–5 minutes until the onion is just tender.
3   Chop the garlic and de-seed and chop the chillies (chilies) finely. Add to the frying pan with the ginger and cumin. Stir for another minute.
4   Cut the tofu into cubes. Toss with the turmeric, then add to the pan, stirring well. Add the tomatoes and water and stir again. Simmer until the mixture is fairly thick, adding a little salt if required.
5   Cook the vermicelli in salted boiling water until just tender, drain, and serve with the tofu mixture poured over.

Tofu, potatoes and cauliflower

Using curry powder instead of the individual spices is a shortcut, but with the piquant flavour of fenugreek seeds, and all the other ingredients, no one will ever guess. Serve with rice.

IMPERIAL/METRIC		AMERICAN
1 small	cauliflower	1 small
2 medium	potatoes	2 medium
1 inch (2.5cm) piece	fresh ginger	1 inch piece
3–4 cloves	garlic	3–4 cloves
1 tbs	water	4 tbs
2	onions	2
2 tbs	vegetable oil	2 tbs
$^1/_2$ tsp	fenugreek seeds	$^1/_2$ tsp
1 inch (2.5cm) piece	cinnamon stick	1 inch piece
2	fresh green chillies (chilies)	2
2	tomatoes	2
2 tsp	curry powder	2 tsp
2 oz (55g)	creamed coconut	$^1/_4$ cup
$^1/_2$ pint (285ml)	hot water	$1^1/_3$ cups
as required	sea salt	as required
$^1/_2$–$^3/_4$ lb (225–340g)	firm tofu	1–$1^1/_2$ cups
1 oz (30g)	vegetable margarine	2 tbs
2 tbs	lemon juice	2 tbs
2 tsp	garam masala	2 tsp

1 Break the cauliflower into florets and cook in salted boiling water for about 1 minute, then drain and rinse in cold water. Set aside.
2 Cook the potatoes in salted boiling water. Drain and cool them, peel if desired, and cut into thick slices.
3 Put the peeled ginger and garlic in a liquidizer or food processor with the water and blend. Chop the onions finely.

4 Heat the oil in a heavy frying pan. Add the fenugreek seeds and the cinnamon stick, and stir. Then add the onions and sauté for 2–3 minutes.

5 Finely chop the chillies (chilis). Add to the frying pan with the ginger/garlic mixture. Stir and fry for another minute.

6 Peel and chop the tomatoes. Add to the frying pan with the curry powder and fry for a further 2 minutes.

7 Combine the creamed coconut and hot water in a liquidizer (or even a glass jar) to make coconut milk. Add to the pan and simmer for about 5 minutes. Add the cauliflower and a little salt, and simmer for a further 5 minutes, with the pan covered.

8 Cut the tofu into large cubes, and sauté in the margarine in a separate pan until golden.

9 Add to the cauliflower mixture along with the potatoes and the lemon juice. Simmer for another 5 minutes.

10 Sprinkle the garam masala over it before serving.

Vegetable kheema

Kheema *in Indian dishes is normally minced meat; here is an animal-free version. It is nice served with chapatis or other Indian bread.*

IMPERIAL/METRIC		AMERICAN
2 large or 4 small	tomatoes	2 large or 4 small
3	fresh chillies (chilies)	3
3 cloves	garlic	3 cloves
1/2 inch (1.25cm) piece	fresh ginger	1/2 inch piece
3	cloves	3
seeds of 3	cardamom pods	seeds of 3
8	black peppercorns	8
2 tsp	cumin seeds	2 tsp
1/2 tsp	chilli (chili) powder	1/2 tsp
3	onions	3
4 tbs	vegetable oil	4 tbs
1 1/2–2 lb (680–900g)	cauliflower	1 1/2–2 lb
1/2 tsp	turmeric	1/2 tsp
1/4 pint (140ml)	water	2/3 cup
6 oz (170g)	firm tofu	3/4 cup
as required	sea salt	as required

1 Peel and chop the tomatoes. Put in a liquidizer with the finely chopped chillies (chilies), garlic and ginger, whole cloves, cardamom seeds, peppercorns, cumin seeds and chilli (chili) powder. Blend very thoroughly.
2 Chop the onions. Sauté in the oil in a saucepan until lightly browned. Add the tomato mixture and continue to cook for 3–4 minutes.
3 Grate the cauliflower. Add to the saucepan with the turmeric and water. Bring to the boil, then lower the heat and simmer for about 10 minutes.
4 Uncover the saucepan and crumble the tofu into it. Stir well, then add salt to taste. Simmer, uncovered, for 3–4 minutes.

Dahl with tofu

The combination of lentils and tofu makes this a particularly high-protein dish. Serve it with brown rice and with mango chutney if desired.

IMPERIAL/METRIC		AMERICAN
2	onions	2
2–3 cloves	garlic	2–3 cloves
2 oz (55g)	vegetable margarine	$\frac{1}{4}$ cup
8	cloves	8
$\frac{1}{2}$ inch (1.25cm) piece	cinnamon stick	$\frac{1}{2}$ inch piece
2 tsp	cumin seeds	2 tsp
2 tsp	coriander seeds	2 tsp
1 tsp	poppy seeds	1 tsp
seeds of 4	cardamom pods	seeds of 4
1 tsp	chilli (chili) powder	1 tsp
2 tsp	turmeric	2 tsp
$\frac{1}{2}$ lb (225g)	red lentils	$1\frac{1}{4}$ cups
$1\frac{1}{2}$ pints (850ml)	water	$3\frac{3}{4}$ cups
$\frac{1}{2}$ lb (225g)	firm tofu	1 cup
1 oz (30g)	creamed coconut	2 tbs
as required	sea salt	as required

1 Chop the onions. Chop the garlic finely. Sauté in half the margarine until lightly browned.
2 Put the cloves, cinnamon, cumin, coriander, poppy seeds and cardamom seeds into a liquidizer or coffee grinder and grind thoroughly.
3 Stir the ground spices into the onions and garlic, along with the chilli (chili) powder and turmeric. Stir well and cook for 1–2 minutes. Stir in the lentils. Add the water, bring to the boil, then lower the heat and simmer for 15–20 minutes.
4 Cut the tofu into cubes. Sauté in a separate pan in the remaining margarine until golden.
5 When the lentils have turned into a thick purée stir in the creamed coconut, the tofu cubes, and salt to taste.

Tofu and peas korma

Serve this dish for a special occasion with brown or pilau rice, papadums or chapatis, and chutney if desired.

IMPERIAL/METRIC		AMERICAN
1 lb (455g)	firm tofu	2 cups
as required	oil for deep-frying	as required
2 large or 4 small	tomatoes	2 large or 4 small
1 oz (30g)	cashew pieces	3 tbs
1 inch (2.5cm) piece	fresh ginger	1 inch piece
4 cloves	garlic	4 cloves
2 large	onions	2 large
2 oz (55g)	vegetable margarine	1/4 cup
2	cinnamon sticks	2
2	bay leaves	2
4	cloves	4
1 tsp	chilli (chili) powder	1 tsp
1/2 pint (285ml)	water	1 1/3 cups
1/2 pint (285ml)	soya (soy) yogurt	1 1/3 cups
2 tsp	cumin seeds	2 tsp
1 tsp	coriander seeds	1 tsp
2 tsp	garam masala	2 tsp
4 oz (115g)	fresh (shelled) or frozen peas	2/3 cup
1 tsp	raw cane sugar	1 tsp
as required	sea salt	as required

1 Cut the tofu into half. Cut one half into small cubes and deep-fry in the oil until golden. Drain and set aside.
2 Peel and chop the tomatoes. Put in a liquidizer with the cashew pieces, chopped ginger and garlic. Blend thoroughly.
3 Grate the onions coarsely. Sauté them in the margarine until lightly browned. Lower the heat, stir in the cinnamon sticks, bay leaves and cloves, and cook for 3–4 minutes longer. Stir in the chilli (chili) powder, then add the water, puréed tomato mixture and the yogurt. Bring to the boil.

4 Grind the cumin and coriander seeds and stir into the mixture with the garam masala. Simmer for a few minutes.
5 Add the deep-fried tofu cubes and the peas and cook for a further 2–3 minutes.
6 Crumble the remaining tofu into the saucepan, along with the sugar, and salt to taste. Heat thoroughly before serving.

Spicy tofu with coconut sauce

Another special-occasion dish. Serve with rice and your choice of accompaniments.

IMPERIAL/METRIC		AMERICAN
1¼–1½ lb (565–680g)	firm tofu	2½–3 cups
2 tbs	coriander seeds	2 tbs
¼ tsp	fenugreek seeds	¼ tsp
1 tsp	black peppercorns	1 tsp
10	dried curry leaves	10
1	onion	1
3 cloves	garlic	3 cloves
2 tbs	vegetable oil	2 tbs
1 tsp	black mustard seeds	1 tsp
1 tsp	finely grated fresh ginger	1 tsp
2 tbs	paprika	2 tbs
¾ tsp	chilli (chili) powder	¾ tsp
½ tsp	turmeric	½ tsp
as required	sea salt	as required
2 tsp	lemon juice	2 tsp
2	fresh green chillies (chilies)	2
¾ pint (425ml)	water	2 cups
6 oz (175g)	creamed coconut	¾ cup

1 Drain the tofu well. Cut into cubes and set aside.
2 Heat a small frying pan over a medium heat, then put in the coriander and fenugreek seeds and the peppercorns. Stir them for about a minute or so until they are lightly roasted. Remove from the heat. Put them in a liquidizer or coffee grinder and grind with the curry leaves as finely as possible.
3 Slice the onion thinly and chop the garlic. Heat the oil in a pan and add the mustard seeds. As soon as they begin to pop add the onion and garlic. Cook over a medium heat until lightly browned. Stir in the ginger, then add the paprika, chilli (chili) powder, turmeric, salt, lemon juice, whole chillies (chilies) and the ground toasted spice mixture. Add the water, bring to the boil, then lower the heat and simmer for 5 minutes.
4 Turn up the heat and add the tofu cubes. Stir them for 2–3 minutes or until they are well heated. Grate the creamed coconut and add it to the pan. Stir it in until completely dissolved.
5 Remove the chillies (chilies) before serving.

Tofu and green pea bhajia

A dairy-free version of a popular Indian dish. Serve with rice or chapatis.

IMPERIAL/METRIC		AMERICAN
1 lb (455g)	medium or firm tofu	2 cups
2 tbs plus additional for deep-frying	vegetable oil	2 tbs plus additional for deep-frying
2	onions	2
3	tomatoes	3
2 cloves	garlic	2 cloves
2	fresh chillies (chilies)	2
¹/₂ inch (1.25cm) piece	fresh ginger	¹/₂ inch piece
2 tsp	coriander seeds	2 tsp
2 tsp	turmeric	2 tsp
¹/₄ tsp	chilli (chili) powder	¹/₄ tsp
as required	sea salt	as required
¹/₂ lb (225g)	fresh (shelled) or frozen peas	1¹/₃ cups

1 Cut the tofu into small cubes and deep-fry in the oil until lightly golden. Drain well.
2 Chop the onions. Fry in the 2 tbs vegetable oil for about 3 minutes.
3 Chop the tomatoes. Crush the garlic. De-seed and chop the chillies (chilies) finely. Peel and chop the ginger finely. Add these ingredients with the coriander seeds, turmeric and chilli (chili) powder to the onions and stir well. Cook for about 5 minutes.
4 Add the fried tofu cubes to the saucepan. Sprinkle a little salt over them and stir well. Cook for about 5 minutes.
5 Add the peas to the saucepan. Cover and cook until they are just tender.

7
Chinese— and other Far Eastern-style Dishes

 # Tofu lo mein

For those who avoid eggs, it is becoming much easier these days to find eggless Chinese noodles (including wholewheat varieties) – or thin Italian pasta could be used instead. As with most of the dishes in this chapter, this one is a complete meal, requiring no accompaniment.

IMPERIAL/METRIC		AMERICAN
¹/₂ lb (225g)	firm tofu	1 cup
1–2 tbs	soy sauce	1–2 tbs
1–2 tbs	cornflour (cornstarch)	1–2 tbs
³/₄ lb (340g)	thin Chinese noodles	³/₄ lb
as required	sesame oil	as required
1 tin (about 14 oz [400g])	bamboo shoots	1 can (14–16 oz)
1 small bunch	spring onions (scallions)	1 small bunch
2 tbs	vegetable oil	2 tbs
¹/₂ lb (225g)	fresh beansprouts	¹/₂ lb
as required	sea salt	as required

1 Cut the tofu into cubes. Sprinkle with the soy sauce and then with the cornflour (cornstarch) and toss well. Set aside.
2 Cook the noodles in salted boiling water until just tender, drain well and run cold water over them. Toss with 1 tbs sesame oil and set aside.
3 Drain the bamboo shoots and slice thinly. Chop the spring onions (scallions).
4 Heat the vegetable oil in a wok or frying pan. Add the tofu and stir-fry for 2–3 minutes. Add the bamboo shoots, lower the heat to medium, and stir-fry for 1–2 minutes. Add the noodles, raise the heat, and cook, stirring constantly, allowing some of the noodles to become browned.
5 Add the beansprouts and stir-fry for 2 minutes. Add the salt, spring onions (scallions), and additional sesame oil to taste, and mix thoroughly. Serve immediately.

Burmese-style kung lo mein

Here is a spicy version of the recipe above.

IMPERIAL/METRIC		AMERICAN
¹/₂ lb (225g)	firm or medium tofu	1 cup
4 tbs plus additional for deep-frying	vegetable oil	4 tbs plus additional for deep-frying
4 cloves	garlic	4 cloves
1 tsp	sesame oil	1 tsp
¹/₂ lb (225g)	spinach	¹/₂ lb
¹/₂ lb (225g)	Chinese cabbage	¹/₂ lb
4	spring onions (scallions)	4
2	fresh chillies (chilies)	2
1¹/₂–2 tbs	soy sauce	1¹/₂–2 tbs
³/₄ lb (340g)	Chinese noodles	³/₄ lb

1 Cut the tofu into cubes and deep-fry in the vegetable oil until golden. Drain and set aside.
2 Chop the garlic finely. Heat the 4 tbs vegetable oil and the sesame oil in a wok or large frying pan until very hot. Drop in the garlic pieces and fry until brown, being careful not to let them burn. Remove and drain on kitchen towels.
3 Chop the spinach and Chinese cabbage coarsely. Chop the spring onions (scallions) and de-seed and chop the chillies (chilies) finely. Put the vegetables into the wok and stir-fry for about 3 minutes, until the spinach has wilted. Add the deep-fried tofu and the soy sauce and mix well.
4 Cook the noodles in salted boiling water until just tender then drain. Toss with the tofu and vegetable mixture. Sprinkle with the crisp garlic bits and serve.

Tofu with almonds

Frozen tofu gives this dish a 'meaty' texture. Serve it with brown rice.

IMPERIAL/METRIC		AMERICAN
1/2 lb (225g)	frozen tofu	1 cup
4 tbs	vegetable oil	4 tbs
4 oz (115g)	blanched whole almonds	1 cup
1	green (bell) pepper	1
1	carrot	1
1 tin (about 10 oz [275g])	bamboo shoots	1 can (10 oz)
1	onion	1
1 1/2 tbs	cornflour (cornstarch)	1 1/2 tbs
2 tsp	raw cane sugar (optional)	2 tsp
1 1/2 tbs	soy sauce	1 1/2 tbs
2 tsp	cider vinegar or wine vinegar	2 tsp
1/2 pint (285ml)	water	1 1/3 cups

1 Defrost the tofu, squeeze, drain and dice it.
2 Heat 1 tbs of the oil in a small frying pan and fry the almonds until golden. Set aside.
3 Chop the vegetables.
4 Heat 2 tbs of the oil in a wok or large frying pan and sauté the onion until transparent. Add the remaining oil and the tofu and vegetables and cook, stirring occasionally, for a few minutes.
5 Blend the cornflour (cornstarch), sugar (if using), soy sauce and vinegar with the water and pour over the tofu and vegetable mixture. Bring to the boil, stirring constantly until it thickens.
6 Add the almonds and serve immediately (with additional soy sauce if required).

Tofu fried rice

Fried rice dishes such as this recipe and the next one are particularly convenient if leftover cooked rice is used. But be very careful that the rice has cooked well before being refrigerated, and that it has been chilled for several hours before use.

IMPERIAL/METRIC		AMERICAN
¾ lb (340g)	brown rice	2 cups
1 lb (455g)	firm tofu	2 cups
1 medium	onion	1 medium
4 tbs plus additional for deep-frying	vegetable oil	4 tbs plus additional for deep-frying
½ lb (225g)	mushrooms	4 cups
½ lb (225g)	fresh (shelled) or frozen peas	1⅓ cups
1 tin (about 10 oz [285g])	sliced bamboo shoots	1 can (10 oz)
4 tbs	Smokey Snaps (soy bakon bits)	4 tbs
as required	soy sauce	as required

1 Cook the rice in salted boiling water until tender.
2 Divide the tofu in half. Cut one half into cubes and deep-fry them in the oil. Drain and set aside.
3 Chop the onion and stir-fry in a wok or frying pan in the 4 tbs oil for 3–4 minutes.
4 Chop the mushrooms, add them to the onion, and stir-fry for a further 3–4 minutes. Add the peas, bamboo shoots, deep-fried tofu cubes, and Smokey Snaps (soy bakon bits). Stir-fry for 2–3 minutes longer.
5 Crumble the other half of the tofu into the vegetables and stir-fry for about 2 minutes. Add the rice and soy sauce to taste, stir-fry the whole mixture until well heated and serve at once.

Stir-fried rice with tempeh and tofu

IMPERIAL/METRIC		AMERICAN
³/₄ lb (340g)	brown rice	2 cups
³/₄ lb (340g)	tempeh	³/₄ lb
2 tbs plus additional for deep-frying	vegetable oil	2 tbs plus additional for deep-frying
¹/₂ lb (225g)	firm or medium tofu	1 cup
2 tsp	turmeric	2 tsp
4	spring onions (scallions)	4
2 cloves	garlic	2 cloves
2 tbs	soy sauce	2 tbs

1   Cook the rice in salted boiling water until tender.
2   Cut the tempeh into cubes and deep-fry in the oil. Drain and set aside.
3   Mash the tofu with the turmeric. Chop the spring onions (scallions) finely.
4   Chop the garlic finely. Heat the 2 tbs oil in a wok or frying pan and add the garlic. Stir-fry for 30 seconds or so until lightly browned.
5   Add all the rest of the ingredients and stir-fry until everything is sizzling hot. Serve immediately.

Tofu with spinach

This requires a specialist ingredient – yellow bean paste (sauce) – available at Oriental shops and now often found at supermarkets as well. It does add a special tang to the dish. Serve with rice or noodles.

IMPERIAL/METRIC		AMERICAN
1¼–1½ lb (565–680g)	medium tofu	2½–3 cups
5 tbs	vegetable oil	5 tbs
4 small or 2 large	leeks	4 small or 2 large
1 lb (455g)	fresh spinach	1 lb
1 tbs	cider vinegar or wine vinegar	1 tbs
1 tbs	soy sauce	1 tbs
¼–½ tsp	Tabasco sauce	¼–½ tsp
1 tbs	yellow bean paste (sauce)	1 tbs

1   Cut the tofu into small dice. Heat 3 tbs of the oil in a wok or frying pan and when hot add the tofu pieces. Stir-fry for about 2 minutes, then transfer from the pan to paper towels to drain.
2   Chop the leeks and spinach. Add the rest of the oil to the pan and add the vegetables. Stir fry for about 3 minutes, covering the wok between stirs if desired.
3   Stir in the vinegar, soy sauce, Tabasco sauce and yellow bean paste (sauce). Add the tofu pieces and stir gently.
4   Serve with brown rice or noodles.

Szechwan-style tofu

This recipe also requires yellow bean paste (sauce), but it is a much spicier dish than the one above. Serve with brown rice. Soy sauce may be added to this dish if desired, but yellow bean paste (sauce) is so salty I have never found it necessary.

IMPERIAL/METRIC		AMERICAN
1 lb (455g)	medium tofu	2 cups
3 tbs	vegetable oil	3 tbs
2	green (bell) peppers	2
2	leeks	2
2	fresh chillies (chilies)	2
1–1¹/₂ tsp	chilli (chili) powder	1–1¹/₂ tsp
1 tbs	cider vinegar or wine vinegar	1 tbs
1 tsp	raw cane sugar	1 tsp
2–3 tbs	yellow bean paste (sauce)	2–3 tbs
2 tsp	sesame oil	2 tsp

1 Cut the tofu into small cubes. Heat 2 tbs of the oil in a wok or frying pan and stir-fry the tofu cubes for 2–3 minutes. Remove from the pan and drain.
2 Slice the green (bell) peppers into strips. Chop the leeks. De-seed and chop the chillies (chilies) finely.
3 Heat the remaining oil and add the vegetables. Stir-fry for about 3 minutes. Add the chilli (chili) powder, vinegar, sugar and yellow bean paste (sauce) and mix well.
4 Return the tofu cubes to the wok and stir-fry the mixture for about 3 minutes longer. Sprinkle with the sesame oil and serve immediately.

Tofu with red chilli (chili) sauce

This is a Westernized adaptation of a traditional Szechwan dish. Serve with brown rice.

IMPERIAL/METRIC		AMERICAN
1	leek	1
2 cloves	garlic	2 cloves
2 tbs	vegetable oil	2 tbs
4 oz (115g)	mushrooms	2 cups
$^1/_2$–1 tsp	chilli (chili) powder	$^1/_2$–1 tsp
$^1/_4$ pint (140ml)	water	$^2/_3$ cup
1 tbs	cider vinegar or wine vinegar	1 tbs
2 tbs	tomato ketchup	2 tbs
1 tbs	soy sauce	1 tbs
1–1$^1/_2$ lb (455–680g)	medium tofu	2–3 cups
1 tbs	cornflour (cornstarch) dissolved in 3 tbs water	1 tbs
2	spring onions (scallions)	2

1 Chop the leek and garlic finely. Heat the oil in a wok or frying pan and add the leek and garlic. Stir-fry for about 30 seconds.
2 Chop the mushrooms and add to the wok. Stir-fry for another 1–2 minutes.
3 Add the chilli (chili) powder, water, vinegar, tomato ketchup and soy sauce, bring to the boil and cook for another minute.
4 Dice the tofu and add to the wok. Stir in the dissolved cornflour (cornstarch) and stir until thickened.
5 Chop the spring onions (scallions) finely and sprinkle over the tofu and sauce. Serve immediately.

Szechwan tofu with peanut sauce

Szechwan cuisine is characterized by hot spicing; to make the dish more authentic increase the amount of cayenne pepper. Serve with brown rice. Vegans who do not eat honey could substitute raw cane sugar for it in this recipe.

IMPERIAL/METRIC		AMERICAN
1 medium	carrot	1 medium
1 inch (2.5cm) piece	fresh ginger	1 inch piece
1 tbs	vegetable oil	1 tbs
1 lb (455g)	medium tofu	2 cups
1 tbs	cider vinegar or wine vinegar	1 tbs
1	spring onion (scallion)	1
2 tbs	peanut butter	2 tbs
1/4 tsp	cayenne pepper	1/4 tsp
2 tbs	sesame oil	2 tbs
2 tbs	honey	2 tbs

1 Slice the carrot into matchsticks. Peel and chop the ginger finely. Heat the vegetable oil in a wok or frying pan, add the carrot and ginger, and stir-fry for 2–3 minutes.
2 Cut the tofu into small pieces. Add to the wok with the vinegar. Cover and leave to simmer for about 3 minutes.
3 Chop the spring onion (scallion) finely and add to the wok. Turn the heat off and leave, covered, for 1–2 minutes.
4 Meanwhile, combine the peanut butter, cayenne pepper, sesame oil and honey in a small bowl, stirring gently until smooth.
5 Add the peanut sauce to the tofu mixture and stir in well.

Mushroom-smothered tofu

Dried mushrooms, which are available at Chinese shops, give this dish a rich and unique flavour. Serve with brown rice.

IMPERIAL/METRIC		AMERICAN
16	dried mushrooms	16
1¼–1½ lb (565–680g)	medium tofu	2½–3 cups
1 inch (2.5cm) piece	fresh ginger	1 inch piece
2	spring onions (scallions)	2
4 tbs	vegetable oil	4 tbs
2 tsp	cider vinegar or wine vinegar	2 tsp
3 tbs	soy sauce	3 tbs
1 tsp	raw cane sugar	1 tsp
1 tbs	sesame oil	1 tbs

1 Cover the mushrooms with boiling water and leave to soak for an hour or more. Drain them (reserving the liquid) and squeeze gently. Remove the stalks and slice the caps.

2 Cut the tofu into squares and then cut the squares into triangles. Set aside.

3 Peel the ginger and chop it and the spring onions (scallions) finely. Heat the vegetable oil in a wok or frying pan. Add the ginger and spring onions (scallions) and stir-fry for 1 minute. Add the vinegar, soy sauce, sugar and mushroom liquid (if less than ⅓ pint [200ml, ¾ cup] then add water to bring it up to that amount). Bring to the boil and add the mushrooms and tofu.

4 Turn gently a few times. Lower the heat, cover and simmer for about 10 minutes, turning once halfway through. By the end of the cooking time there should be little or no liquid remaining. Add the sesame oil and serve immediately.

Moo goo gai pan

This Chinese dish – served with rice – is traditionally made with chicken; here is a version requiring no animal ingredients.

IMPERIAL/METRIC		AMERICAN
2	onions	2
4 sticks	celery	4 sticks
4 oz (115g)	mushrooms	2 cups
1	green or red (bell) pepper	1
1 tin (about 10 oz [275g])	water chestnuts	1 can (10 oz)
4–6 oz (115–170g)	Chinese cabbage	1–1^1/$_2$ cups
^{3}/$_4$–1 lb (340–455g)	medium or firm tofu	1^1/$_2$–2 cups
3 tbs	soy sauce	3 tbs
1–2 oz (30–55g)	fresh ginger	1–2 oz
2–3 cloves	garlic	2–3 cloves
6 tbs	vegetable oil	6 tbs
2 tbs	arrowroot	2 tbs
^{3}/$_4$ pint (425ml)	water	2 cups
4 tbs	cider vinegar or wine vinegar	4 tbs
as required	sea salt	as required
4 oz (115g)	fresh beansprouts	2 cups

1 Slice the onions thinly. Chop the celery and mushrooms; cut the green or red (bell) pepper into slivers. Slice the water chestnuts and Chinese cabbage.
2 Dice the tofu. Sprinkle the soy sauce over it, put on to a grill (broiler) pan, and grill (broil) under a medium heat for a few minutes on each side. Set aside.
3 Peel the ginger and chop it and the garlic finely. Sauté in 4 tbs of the oil in a small pan over a medium heat for about 3 minutes.
4 Mix the arrowroot with 2 tbs of the water, the vinegar, and salt. Pour the remainder of the water over the ginger and garlic, and bring to the boil. Turn down to a simmer, then slowly stir in the arrowroot mixture until thickened.
5 Heat the remaining oil in a wok or large frying pan. Add the onions, celery, mushrooms and pepper, and stir-fry for about 5 minutes. Add the Chinese

cabbage, water chestnuts and beansprouts, and stir-fry for a further 3–5 minutes.

6   Add the tofu to the vegetable mixture and stir well. Then pour over the ginger/garlic sauce, and stir over a low heat until well mixed.

 # *Tofu foo yung*

A foo yung is traditionally a scrambled egg mixture; mashed tofu makes a splendid cholesterol-free version. Serve with brown rice, with additional soy sauce if desired.

IMPERIAL/METRIC		AMERICAN
1	onion	1
2	spring onions (scallions)	2
1/2 lb (225g)	mushrooms	4 cups
2 tbs	vegetable oil	2 tbs
12–14 oz (340–400g)	firm or medium tofu	1 1/2–1 3/4 cups
1 tsp	turmeric	1 tsp
as required	sea salt	as required
1 tbs	soy sauce	1 tbs
1/2 lb (225g)	beansprouts	1/2 lb

1   Chop the onion, spring onions (scallions) and mushrooms finely. Heat the oil in a frying pan and stir-fry the vegetables until tender.
2   Mash the tofu, mix well with the turmeric and add to the frying pan, stirring well. Add the salt and soy sauce while stirring. Finally, add the beansprouts and continue stir-frying until they are just wilted.

Steamed tofu and carrots with hot tahini sauce

An exotic combination of flavours, but simple to make.

IMPERIAL/METRIC		AMERICAN
1–1$^{1}/_{4}$ lb (455–565g)	medium tofu	2–2$^{1}/_{2}$ cups
$^{1}/_{2}$ lb (225g)	carrots	$^{1}/_{2}$ lb
4–5 tbs	tahini	4–5 tbs
4–5 tbs	sesame oil	4–5 tbs
3–4 tbs	soy sauce	3–4 tbs
3 tsp	cider vinegar or wine vinegar	3 tsp
3 tsp	Chinese chilli (chili) sauce	3 tsp
4 tbs	water	4 tbs
2 tsp	raw cane sugar	2 tsp

1 Cut the tofu into cubes. Slice the carrots diagonally into matchsticks. Steam the tofu and carrots together for a few minutes until the carrots are just tender.
2 Combine the tahini, sesame oil, soy sauce, vinegar, chilli (chili) sauce, water and sugar in a small saucepan. Heat gently, stirring constantly until smooth.
3 Serve the tofu and carrots on brown rice, topped with the sauce.

Braised tofu

This method of preparing tofu gives it an entirely new texture and a rich flavour. Unlike most of the recipes in this chapter it is not a complete meal: serve it with a seasonal mixture of stir-fried vegetables, preferably with brown rice.

IMPERIAL/METRIC		AMERICAN
1–1¹/₂ lb (455–680g)	medium tofu	2–3 cups
3 tbs	vegetable oil	3 tbs
1 tbs	finely grated fresh ginger	1 tbs
2 tsp	raw cane sugar	2 tsp
3 tbs	soy sauce	3 tbs
¹/₄ pint (140ml)	water	²/₃ cup

1. Dice the tofu into 4–6 squares. Put the squares into a saucepan and cover with water by about 2 inch/5cm. Bring to the boil over a medium heat and simmer for half an hour. Cool, then drain. Cut each square into 8 cubes and press on them gently to remove excess water.
2. Heat the oil in a pan over a medium heat and add the ginger and the tofu cubes. Stir-fry for 1–2 minutes, then stir in the sugar, soy sauce and water. Cover and bring to the boil, then lower the heat and simmer for about an hour, basting occasionally, until most or all of the liquid has been absorbed.

Sweet and sour tofu balls

A lovely combination of flavours and textures. Serve with brown rice.

IMPERIAL/METRIC		AMERICAN
1 lb (455g)	medium or firm tofu	2 cups
1/2 tsp	sea salt	1/2 tsp
2 tbs	wholewheat flour	2 tbs
as required	vegetable oil for deep-frying	as required
4 oz (115g)	fresh or tinned (canned) pineapple in its own juice	4 oz
1	green (bell) pepper	1
2	spring onions (scallions)	2
5 tbs	cider vinegar or wine vinegar	5 tbs
3–4 tbs	raw cane sugar	3–4 tbs
2–3 tbs	soy sauce	2–3 tbs
1 tbs	cornflour (cornstarch) dissolved in 1/3 pint (200ml, 1/3 cup) pineapple juice	1 tbs

1 If using medium tofu wrap it in a clean tea towel (dish towel) or paper towel and leave to drain for half an hour or more. Put the drained tofu into a mixing bowl, mash well, and stir in the salt and flour. Form into small balls and deep-fry in the oil until golden brown. Drain well.

2 Chop the pineapple. Slice the green (bell) pepper into thin slivers. Chop the spring onions (scallions) finely.

3 Put the vinegar, sugar, soy sauce, and cornflour (cornstarch) dissolved in pineapple juice into a wok or large saucepan and bring to the boil gently, stirring constantly until thickened.

4 Add the tofu balls, pineapple, green (bell) pepper and spring onions (scallions), and simmer to heat through for 2–3 minutes. Serve immediately.

Ma po tofu with noodles

When this dish appears on the menu at a Chinese restaurant it is not normally vegetarian, but here is a meat-free version. Traditionally it is served with rice, but I like it with noodles.

IMPERIAL/METRIC		AMERICAN
2 small	leeks	2 small
4 cloves	garlic	4 cloves
2 tbs	vegetable oil	2 tbs
1–1½ lb (455–680g)	medium tofu	2–3 cups
½ pint (285ml)	water or vegetable stock	1⅓ cups
2 tsp	Chinese chilli (chili) sauce	2 tsp
2 tbs	soy sauce	2 tbs
1 tsp	freshly ground black pepper	1 tsp
3 oz (85g)	Smokey Snaps (soy bakon bits)	½ cup
¾ lb (340g)	Chinese noodles	¾ lb
1 tbs	cornflour (cornstarch) dissolved in 2 tbs water	1 tbs
1 tbs	sesame oil	1 tbs

1 Chop the leeks and garlic finely. Heat the vegetable oil in a wok or frying pan, and stir-fry the leeks and garlic for 3–4 minutes.
2 Dice the tofu. Stir into the leeks and garlic. Add the water or stock, the chilli (chili) sauce, soy sauce, black pepper and Smokey Snaps (soy bakon bits). Bring to the boil, then lower the heat and simmer for about 10 minutes.
3 Cook the noodles in salted boiling water until just tender then drain.
4 Add the dissolved cornflour (cornstarch) to the tofu mixture and stir well until thickened. Serve the noodles topped with the sauce, and sprinkle with the sesame oil before serving.

Spiced pressed tofu

Using frozen tofu provides a shortcut to making this traditional Chinese ingredient. The spiced pressed tofu in this recipe is then used in the three recipes that follow. Serve them with brown rice. Five-spice powder is available at Oriental shops.

IMPERIAL/METRIC		AMERICAN
1–1¼ lb (455–565g)	frozen tofu	2–2½ cups
2 large cloves	garlic	2 large cloves
2 tbs	raw cane sugar	2 tbs
2 tsp	vegetable oil	2 tsp
4 tbs	soy sauce	4 tbs
1 tsp	five-spice powder	1 tsp

1. Defrost the tofu, squeeze it to remove the liquid, and cut it into thin strips.
2. Crush the garlic. Put it into a saucepan with the sugar, oil, soy sauce and five-spice powder, and heat gently for about 2–3 minutes.
3. Add the tofu strips and cook for a further 2–3 minutes. Remove from the heat and either use immediately or cool and then refrigerate for up to 2 weeks.

Carrots and celery with spiced pressed tofu

IMPERIAL/METRIC		AMERICAN
½ lb (225g)	carrots	½ lb
6 sticks	celery	6 sticks
3 tbs	vegetable oil	3 tbs
1–1¼ lb (455–565g)	spiced pressed tofu (see above)	2–2½ cups
1½ tbs	cider vinegar or wine vinegar	1½ tbs
1 tbs	sesame oil	1 tbs

1 Slice the carrots and celery into matchsticks.
2 Heat the vegetable oil in a wok or frying pan and stir-fry the carrots and celery for 4–5 minutes, until crisp-tender.
3 Add the spiced pressed tofu and heat thoroughly. Sprinkle in the vinegar and sesame oil and serve immediately.

 # Cabbage with spiced pressed tofu

IMPERIAL/METRIC		AMERICAN
1 lb (155g)	spiced pressed tofu (see page 130)	1 lb
1¼ lb (565g)	cabbage	1¼ lb
1 tsp	sea salt	1 tsp
2 tbs	sesame oil	2 tbs
1 tsp	raw cane sugar	1 tsp
4 tbs	soy sauce	4 tbs
pinch	five-spice powder	pinch

1 Cut the tofu into small cubes. Set aside.
2 Shred the cabbage coarsely. Bring a saucepan of water to the boil, sprinkle in the salt, then plunge the cabbage into the water and cook for 2 minutes. Drain thoroughly.
3 Combine the sesame oil, sugar, soy sauce and five-spice powder in a wok or frying pan. Add the cabbage and mix thoroughly over a gentle heat. Finally, stir in the tofu cubes, heat through and serve immediately.

Cabbage and Chinese mushrooms with spiced pressed tofu

IMPERIAL/METRIC		AMERICAN
6–8 (about 1 oz/30g)	dried Chinese mushrooms	6–8 (about 1 oz)
1–2	fresh chillies (chilies)	1–2
2–3	spring onions (scallions)	2–3
1/2 lb (225g)	cabbage	1/2 lb
2 cloves	garlic	2 cloves
2 tbs	vegetable oil	2 tbs
2 tsp	finely chopped fresh ginger	2 tsp
1 tbs	cider vinegar or wine vinegar	1 tbs
1 tbs	soy sauce	1 tbs
2 tsp	sesame oil	2 tsp
1 lb (455g)	spiced pressed tofu (see page 130)	1 lb

1. Cover the dried mushrooms with hot water and leave to soak for about half an hour.
2. Chop the chillies (chilies) finely (making certain all seeds are removed). Chop the spring onions (scallions). Drain and chop the mushrooms, discarding the stalks. Set aside.
3. Chop the cabbage. Set aside.
4. Crush the garlic. Heat the vegetable oil in a wok or frying pan and add the ginger and garlic. Stir-fry for 30–45 seconds until very lightly browned. Add the spring onions (scallions), chillies (chilies) and mushrooms. Stir-fry for a further 30 seconds.
5. Add the chopped cabbage to the wok. Stir-fry for 1–2 minutes. Add the vinegar, then the soy sauce and sesame oil, and finally the strips of pressed tofu. Continue stir-frying until the cabbage is completely wilted, and serve immediately.

Peking noodles

In this Chinese noodle dish frozen tofu adds a 'meaty' texture. Hoisin sauce is available at Oriental shops and, increasingly, at supermarkets.

IMPERIAL/METRIC		AMERICAN
1 lb (455g)	frozen tofu	2 cups
2 tsp	yeast extract	2 tsp
$^1/_4$ pint (140ml) plus 6 tbs	water	$^2/_3$ cup plus 6 tbs
4	spring onions (scallions)	4
$^1/_2$	cucumber	$^1/_2$
$^1/_2$ lb (225g)	beansprouts	$^1/_2$ lb
2 cloves	garlic	2 cloves
2 tbs	vegetable oil	2 tbs
3 tbs	Hoisin sauce	3 tbs
2 tsp	soy sauce	2 tsp
1 tbs	cider vinegar or wine vinegar	1 tbs
$^3/_4$ lb (340g)	thin noodles	$^3/_4$ lb

1   Defrost the tofu and squeeze well. Dissolve the yeast extract in the 1/4 pint (140ml, 2/3 cup) water in a small saucepan. Crumble the tofu into this and simmer for 1–2 minutes (the liquid should be completely absorbed). Set aside.
2   Chop 2 of the spring onions (scallions) finely. Coarsely grate the cucumber. Mix these ingredients together with the beansprouts and set aside.
3   Chop the garlic finely. Stir-fry in the oil in a wok or large frying pan with the tofu for 1–2 minutes.
4   Chop the remaining 2 spring onions (scallions) finely and add them to the wok, along with the Hoisin sauce, soy sauce, vinegar, and 6 tbs water. Simmer this mixture briefly. Meanwhile cook the noodles in salted boiling water until just tender.
5   Serve the noodles with the tofu sauce poured over them, topped with the mixture of beansprouts, cucumber and spring onions (scallions).

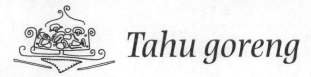

Tahu goreng

Tofu is known as tahu *in Indonesia, where it forms the main ingredient of various dishes.* Goreng *just means fried, and* tahu goreng *can simply be slices of deep-fried tofu or it can be a spicy dish like this one.*

IMPERIAL/METRIC		AMERICAN
1¹/₄ lb (565g)	medium or firm tofu	2¹/₂ cups
as required	cornflour (cornstarch)	as required
as required	vegetable oil for deep-frying	as required
³/₄ lb (340g)	beansprouts	³/₄ lb
¹/₂	cucumber	¹/₂
2	fresh chillies (chilies)	2
3 cloves	garlic	3 cloves
3	spring onions (scallions)	3
2 tbs	lemon juice	2 tbs
4 tbs	soy sauce	4 tbs
1 tbs	raw cane sugar	1 tbs
as required	cooked brown rice	as required

1 Dice the tofu. Spread cornflour (cornstarch) out on a plate and roll the tofu cubes in it. Deep-fry the cubes in the oil and set aside (keep warm if desired).
2 Blanch the beansprouts in boiling water for 1 minute, then drain and pour cold water over them. Drain well. Slice the cucumber into thin matchsticks.
3 Chop the chillies (chilies), garlic and spring onions (scallions) and put in a liquidizer with the lemon juice, soy sauce and sugar. Blend thoroughly.
4 Arrange the beansprouts, cucumber and fried tofu cubes on a bed of cooked rice. Pour the sauce over this and serve immediately.

Fried tofu with peanuts

This Indonesian dish – and the one that follows – uses sambal oelek, *a spicy condiment which can add zest to other dishes as well. It is becoming increasingly available in delicatessens, but if it cannot be found Tabasco sauce could be substituted; use double the amount.*

IMPERIAL/METRIC		AMERICAN
1 lb (455g)	medium tofu	2 cups
1 tbs plus additional for deep-frying	vegetable oil	1 tbs plus additional for deep-frying
2 cloves	garlic	2 cloves
6 oz (170g)	plain dry-roasted peanuts (available at some wholefood shops or wash salt off ordinary roasted peanuts)	1 cup
2 tbs	soy sauce	2 tbs
2 tbs	cider vinegar or wine vinegar	2 tbs
1/2 tsp	*sambal oelek*	1/2 tsp
1 tsp	dark muscavado sugar	1 tsp
1/4 pint (140ml)	coconut milk (or just under 1 pint [140ml, 2/3 cup] water and 1/2 oz [15g] creamed coconut)	2/3 cup
4 oz (115g)	white cabbage	1 cup
3 oz (85g)	fresh beansprouts	1 1/2 cups
4	spring onions (scallions)	4

1 Dice the tofu. Deep-fry in the oil until golden brown then drain.
2 Crush the garlic and sauté in the tbs oil over a low heat, stirring constantly, for 1–2 minutes.
3 Grind half the peanuts and add to the garlic, along with the soy sauce, vinegar, sambal oelek and sugar. Stir until well mixed. Gradually add the coconut milk (or water and creamed coconut) and stir until the sauce is a thick pouring consistency.
4 Shred the cabbage finely.
5 Put the tofu on a serving dish, cover with the cabbage and then with the beansprouts. Spoon the sauce over.

6   Chop the spring onions (scallions) finely. Sprinkle over the top of the sauce along with the whole peanuts.

Fried tofu with soy sauce

IMPERIAL/METRIC		AMERICAN
³/₄–1 lb (340–455g)	medium tofu	1¹/₂–2 cups
as required	oil for deep frying	as required
4	spring onions (scallions)	4
4 oz (115g)	fresh beansprouts	2 cups
1	onion	1
1 clove	garlic	1 clove
2¹/₂ tbs	soy sauce	2¹/₂ tbs
1 tbs	muscavado or other dark raw cane sugar	1 tbs
1 tsp	*sambal oelek*	1 tsp

1   Dice the tofu and deep-fry in the oil until golden. Drain, then arrange on a dish.
2   Chop the spring onions (scallions) finely.
3   Cover the tofu with the beansprouts and sprinkle with the spring onions.
4   Chop the onion coarsely. Chop the garlic finely. Put the soy sauce, sugar, onion, garlic and sambal oelek into a liquidizer and blend thoroughly.
5   Pour this mixture over the rest and serve.

Gado-gado

This is probably the best-known Indonesian dish of them all. There are innumerable variations.

IMPERIAL/METRIC		AMERICAN
1 lb (455g)	firm tofu	2 cups
3 tbs	vegetable oil	3 tbs
1	onion	1
2–3 cloves	garlic	2–3 cloves
1/2 pint (285ml)	hot water	1 1/3 cups
1/2 lb (225g)	crunchy peanut butter	1 cup
2 tsp	dark muscavado sugar	2 tsp
1/2 tsp	*sambal oelek* or	1/2 tsp
1 tsp	Tabasco sauce	1 tsp
juice and rind of 1	lemon	juice and rind of 1
1 tbs	grated fresh ginger	1 tbs
1/4 pint (140ml)	coconut milk (or 1–2 oz [30–55g] creamed coconut diluted with 1/3 pint [200ml, 3/4 cup] hot water)	2/3 cup
1/2 lb (225g)	shredded cabbage	1/2 lb
1/2 lb (225g)	green beans	1/2 lb
1/2 lb (225g)	fresh beansprouts	1/2 lb
1/4	cucumber	1/4

1 Cut the tofu into cubes and sauté in 2 tbs of the oil until golden brown. Remove from the heat.
2 Chop the onion and garlic finely and fry in the remaining oil until lightly browned.
3 Stir the hot water and peanut butter into the onion and garlic and stir over a low heat until the peanut butter has melted. Add the sugar, sambal oelek or Tabasco sauce, lemon juice and rind, ginger and coconut milk, stirring well until thoroughly blended.
4 Blanch the cabbage and green beans in salted boiling water (the beansprouts may be blanched or served raw). Slice the cucumber. Arrange the vegetables on a plate, top with the tofu cubes and pour the sauce over the whole.

 # Teriyaki tofu

This is a Westernized version of a traditional Japanese style of cookery. It could be served with rice and stir-fried vegetables, or Western-style with a baked potato and salad or cooked seasonal vegetables, or even as an open sandwich for a light lunch. (Vegans who don't eat honey could substitute raw cane sugar for it here.)

IMPERIAL/METRIC		AMERICAN
1 lb (455g)	firm tofu	2 cups
¼ pint (140ml)	soy sauce	⅔ cup
¼ pint (140ml)	water	⅔ cup
1–2 tbs	honey	1–2 tbs
2 tsp	ground ginger	2 tsp
½ tsp	garlic salt	½ tsp
3 tsp	sesame oil	3 tsp
2 tsp	mustard	2 tsp
as required	freshly ground black pepper	as required

1 Cut the tofu into 8–12 slices and set aside.
2 In a small bowl, combine the soy sauce, water, honey, ginger, garlic salt, sesame oil and mustard, and mix well with a fork. Grind in a little black pepper.
3 Place the tofu slices in a shallow bowl or bowls and pour the marinade over them. Cover and leave to marinate in the refrigerator for at least an hour, turning once or twice, if possible, during that time.
4 Remove the tofu slices from the marinade and drain them briefly on paper towels. Then put them under a hot grill (broiler) and grill (broil) for 3–4 minutes on each side.

Malay vermicelli

Tofu is also found in Malaysian dishes. This is a rich, aromatic mixture.

IMPERIAL/METRIC		AMERICAN
2 tsp	coriander seeds	2 tsp
seeds from 2	cardamom pods	seeds from 2
2 tsp	cumin seeds	2 tsp
2 tsp	turmeric	2 tsp
1/2 tsp	ground cinnamon	1/2 tsp
pinch	ground cloves	pinch
2 tsp	ground fenugreek	2 tsp
4	onions	4
4	tomatoes	4
3/4–1 lb (340–455g)	firm tofu	1 1/2–2 cups
2 oz (55g)	vegetable margarine	1/4 cup
3 cloves	garlic	3 cloves
2 tsp	sea salt	2 tsp
2 tsp	chilli (chili) powder	2 tsp
1 tbs	finely chopped ginger	1 tbs
1/4 pint (140ml)	water	2/3 cup
juice of 1	lemon	juice of 1
3/4 lb (340g)	vermicelli	3/4 lb
1–2 tbs	chopped parsley	1–2 tbs

1 Heat all the spices in a dry heavy frying pan until aromatic, then grind in a mortar or blender until pulverized.
2 Chop the onions coarsely, then blend in a liquidizer. Peel and chop the tomatoes. Dice the tofu.
3 Melt the margarine in a pan, add the puréed onion and sauté, stirring until lightly browned. Add the tomatoes and fry for 1–2 minutes, then add the diced tofu and stir-fry for a further 2–3 minutes.
4 Crush the garlic and add to the saucepan, along with the salt, chilli (chili) powder, ginger and the spice mixture, stirring well.

5   Add a little of the water and simmer over a low heat for a few minutes. Then stir in the rest of the water and the lemon juice and leave to simmer for about 5 minutes longer.
6   Boil the vermicelli until just tender and drain.
7   Toss the tofu mixture with the vermicelli and garnish with the parsley.

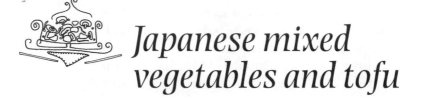

Japanese mixed vegetables and tofu

In contrast to Indonesian and Malaysian cuisine, the Japanese – also great users of tofu – prefer more delicate flavours. Serve this with brown rice.

IMPERIAL/METRIC		AMERICAN
6 oz (170g)	medium tofu	$^3/_4$ cup
1 small	aubergine (eggplant)	1 small
as required	sea salt	as required
1 clove	garlic	1 clove
1	onion	1
2 tbs plus additional for deep-frying	vegetable oil	2 tbs plus additional for deep-frying
4 oz (115g)	cabbage	4 oz
4 oz (115g)	broccoli	4 oz
4 oz (115g)	green beans	4 oz
1	green (bell) pepper	1
2 sticks	celery	2 sticks
2 oz (55g)	mushrooms	1 cup
$^1/_2$ tin (5 oz [140g])	sliced bamboo shoots	$^1/_2$ can (5 oz)
$^1/_4$ pint (140ml)	water	$^2/_3$ cup
1 tsp	freshly ground black pepper	1 tsp
2 tbs	soy sauce	2 tbs

1 Dice the tofu and deep-fry it in the oil. Drain and set aside.
2 Slice the aubergine (eggplant) thinly. Salt the slices; leave with a weight on them for about half an hour, then rinse and pat dry.
3 Crush the garlic. Slice the onion thinly. Heat the 2 tbs oil in a wok or large frying pan and sauté the onion and garlic until lightly browned.
4 Chop the cabbage coarsely. Cut the broccoli into florets. Slice the beans, green (bell) pepper, celery and mushrooms. Add these vegetables to the onion and garlic, along with the aubergine (eggplant) and bamboo shoots, and stir-fry for 3–5 minutes. Add the water, black pepper and soy sauce, bring to the boil, then reduce the heat and simmer for 5–10 minutes. Add the tofu and simmer for a further 5–10 minutes before serving.

8
Desserts

Calling something cheesecake that has no cheese in it may seem strange, but the texture is so similar to traditional cheesecake that it could hardly be called anything else. Below are three delicious versions, any of which would make a fine finish to a dinner party.

Tofu cheesecake 1

IMPERIAL/METRIC		AMERICAN
¹/₂ lb (225g)	granola (e.g. Jordan's Crunchy Cereal or similar)	2 cups
3–4 oz (85–115g)	vegetable margarine	¹/₃–¹/₂ cup
¹/₃ pint (200ml)	soya (soy) milk	³/₄ cup
1¹/₄ lb (565g)	firm tofu	2¹/₂ cups
8 tbs	vegetable oil	¹/₂ cup
1 tsp	vanilla essence	1 tsp
1 tsp	almond essence	1 tsp
2 tsp	arrowroot	2 tsp
as required	fruit topping (e.g. fresh strawberries or cherries, stewed fruit thickened with a little arrowroot, 'runny' raw cane sugar jam, etc.)	as required

1 Grind the granola until very fine. Melt the margarine and mix in the granola crumbs. Spread in a greased flat tin and bake in the oven at 350°F (180°C, Gas Mark 4) for 5 minutes.
2 Put the milk, tofu, oil, vanilla essence, almond essence and arrowroot into a liquidizer and blend thoroughly until smooth (this will probably need to be done in two or three batches). Remove the crumb crust from the oven and pour in the filling.
3 Bake in the oven at the same temperature for 20 minutes. Remove and leave to cool. Top with fruit topping and chill before serving.

Tofu cheesecake 2

IMPERIAL/METRIC		AMERICAN
	Base:	
4 oz (115g)	wholewheat flour	1 cup
1 oz (30g)	raw cane sugar	2 tbs
pinch	sea salt	pinch
pinch	cinnamon	pinch
2 oz (55g)	vegetable margarine	1/4 cup
1 tbs	water	1 tbs
	Filling:	
10 oz (285g)	firm tofu	1 1/4 cups
2 tbs	vegetable oil	2 tbs
2 oz (55g)	raw cane sugar	4 tbs
juice and rind of 1	lemon	juice and rind of 1
1 tsp	vanilla essence	1 tsp
1 1/2 oz (45g)	ground almonds	1/3 cup
2 oz (55g)	raisins or sultanas	1/3 cup
	(golden seedless raisins)	

1 To make the base, mix the flour, sugar, salt and cinnamon together in a bowl. Rub the margarine in finely. Finally, work in the water. Transfer the mixture to an oiled flan tin and pat down lightly. Bake in the oven for 10 minutes at 350°F (180°C, Gas Mark 4).

2 Meanwhile, put the tofu, oil, sugar, lemon juice and rind, and vanilla essence into a liquidizer or food processor and blend thoroughly. Stir in the ground almonds and raisins.

3 Remove the base from the oven and spoon the filling evenly over the top. Return to the oven and bake for 30 minutes. Cool, then chill before serving.

Raspberry tofu cheesecake

This recipe contains honey.

IMPERIAL/METRIC		AMERICAN
1 1/2 oz (45g)	rolled oats	1/3 cup
1/2 oz (15g)	desiccated (shredded) coconut	1/6 cup
1 tbs	vegetable margarine	1 tbs
3/4 lb (340g)	firm tofu	1 1/2 cups
2 tbs	soya (soy) yogurt	2 tbs
2 tbs	raw cane sugar	2 tbs
juice and rind of 1/2	orange	juice and rind of 1/2
1/2 tsp	vanilla essence	1/2 tsp
2 tsp	tahini	2 tsp
pinch	sea salt	pinch
2–3 tbs	honey	2–3 tbs
4 tbs	water	4 tbs
1/8 tsp	powdered agar-agar	1/8 tsp
4 oz (115g)	fresh or defrosted frozen raspberries	4 oz

1   Mix the oats and coconut together. Spread the margarine over the bottom of a flan tin, then sprinkle the oat and coconut mixture over it. Set aside.
2   Combine the tofu, yogurt, sugar, orange juice and rind, vanilla essence, tahini and salt in a liquidizer. Blend thoroughly. Pour into the flan case.
3   Melt the honey in the water in a small pan over a medium heat and dissolve the agar-agar in it. Bring to the boil then simmer for about 1 minute. Remove from the heat and stir in the raspberries. Pour over the tofu mixture in the flan tin.
4   Bake in the oven at 350°F (180°C, Gas Mark 4) for 35 minutes. Chill for several hours before serving.

Roshmalay

Most Indian sweets are based on dairy products, but here is a dairy-free version of an exotic treat.

IMPERIAL/METRIC		AMERICAN
1 lb (455g)	medium or firm tofu	2 cups
3/4 pint (425ml)	soya (soy) milk	2 cups
1 oz (30g)	vegetable margarine	2 tbs
6	cardamom pods	6
2 oz (55g)	flaked (slivered) almonds	1/2 cup
1/8 tsp	freshly ground nutmeg	1/8 tsp
4–6 oz (115–170g)	raw cane sugar	3/4–1 cup
2 tsp	rosewater	2 tsp
1/2 tsp	vanilla essence	1/2 tsp
8 tbs	water	8 tbs

1   Put the tofu into a clean tea towel (dish towel) and squeeze until as much liquid as possible has been removed. Place the tofu in a mixing bowl and knead briefly. Form into small balls about the size of walnuts and set aside.

2   Bring the milk and margarine to the boil in a saucepan. Remove the seeds from the cardamoms, grind them and add to the saucepan with the almonds, nutmeg, and half the sugar. Turn the heat down to fairly low and simmer, uncovered, for 10–15 minutes. Remove from the heat, add the rosewater and vanilla essence, and leave to cool.

3   In a small saucepan combine the water and the remaining sugar, bring to the boil, and cook uncovered over a medium heat for about 15 minutes. Dip the tofu balls into this syrup and place on a plate to cool.

4   Put the tofu balls into serving bowls, pour the milk mixture over them and chill thoroughly until ready to serve.

Apricot triangles

This is a light pastry dessert.

IMPERIAL/METRIC		AMERICAN
4 oz (115g)	vegetable margarine	$1/2$ cup
$1/2$ lb (225g)	firm tofu	1 cup
$1/4$ tsp	sea salt	$1/4$ tsp
4–5 oz (115–140g)	81% (or 85%) wholewheat flour	1–$1^1/_4$ cups
as required	apricot jam	as required
as required	icing (powdered) sugar or finely ground raw cane sugar	as required

1　Combine the margarine, tofu and salt in a bowl and mix well with a wooden spoon.
2　Add the flour and knead until a soft dough is formed. Cover and chill.
3　Roll the dough out and cut into small squares. In the centre of each square put about 1 teaspoon apricot jam. Fold the dough over to form a triangle and press the edges together to seal. Prick with a fork, and bake in the oven on an oiled baking sheet at 375°F (190°C, Gas Mark 5) for half an hour.
4　Remove the triangles from the oven, sprinkle the tops with icing (powdered) sugar or finely ground raw cane sugar and serve warm.

Pashka 1

For this traditional Russian Easter dish, tofu is used instead of cottage cheese to make a delightful dessert.

IMPERIAL/METRIC		AMERICAN
$^1/_2$–$^3/_4$ lb (225–340g)	firm tofu	1–1$^1/_2$ cups
2 oz (55g)	vegetable margarine	$^1/_4$ cup
4–5 tbs	soya (soy) yogurt	4–5 tbs
2 oz (55g)	raw cane sugar	4 tbs
2 oz (55g)	ground almonds	$^1/_2$ cup
2 oz (55g)	finely chopped mixed candied peel	$^1/_3$ cup
3 oz (85g)	raisins	$^1/_2$ cup
$^1/_2$ tsp	vanilla essence	$^1/_2$ tsp

1 Put the tofu into a clean tea towel (dish towel) and squeeze well to extract as much liquid as possible.
2 Put the squeezed tofu into a mixing bowl and cream the margarine into it. Mix in all the rest of the ingredients.
3 Spoon the mixture into 1 large or 4 small serving dishes, press down firmly, cover and chill for several hours before serving.

Pashka 2

This is a less elaborate version than the one above.

IMPERIAL/METRIC		AMERICAN
$^1/_2$–$^3/_4$ lb (225–340g)	firm tofu	1–1$^1/_2$ cups
2 oz (55g)	raw cane sugar	4 tbs
2 oz (55g)	ground almonds	$^1/_2$ cup
4–5 tsp	soya (soy) yogurt	4–5 tsp
juice and rind of 1	lemon	juice and rind of 1
3 oz (85g)	raisins and/or sultanas (golden seedless raisins)	$^1/_2$ cup

1 Put the tofu into a clean tea towel (dish towel) and squeeze well to extract as much liquid as possible.
2 Combine with all the other ingredients and serve.

'Creamy' pies are not only a treat to eat, they are also convenient as they can be made many hours in advance of a meal. Below are four versions.

Tofu pie

IMPERIAL/METRIC		AMERICAN
$^1/_2$ tsp	powdered agar-agar	$^1/_2$ tsp
$^1/_4$ pint (140ml)	water	$^2/_3$ cup
6 oz (170g)	broken cashews	$1^1/_3$ cups
$^1/_2$ lb (225g)	medium tofu	1 cup
$^1/_2$ pint (285ml)	soya (soy) yogurt	$1^1/_3$ cups
4 tsp	lemon juice	4 tsp
2 tsp	vanilla essence	2 tsp
4 tbs	raw cane sugar	4 tbs
1	pre-baked wholewheat pastry shell (made from 4–6 oz [115–170g, 1–$1^1/_2$ cups] flour and 2–3 oz [55–85g, $^1/_4$–$^1/_3$ cup] vegetable margarine)	1
as required	fresh strawberries	as required

1 Dissolve the agar-agar in the water in a small pan, bring to the boil and simmer for 1 minute.
2 Put the cashews in a food processor and grind until fine. Add the agar-agar mixture, along with the tofu, yogurt, lemon juice, vanilla essence and sugar. Blend thoroughly.
3 Pour into the pie shell. Chill thoroughly. Top with strawberries before serving.

Chocolate-topped pie

IMPERIAL/METRIC		AMERICAN
4 oz (115g)	wholewheat flour	1 cup
pinch	sea salt	pinch
2 oz (55g)	vegetable margarine	¹/₄ cup
³/₄ lb (340g)	medium tofu	1¹/₂ cups
3 oz (85g)	raw cane sugar	¹/₂ cup
1¹/₂ tsp	vanilla essence	1¹/₂ tsp
1 tbs	vegetable oil	1 tbs
1¹/₂ oz (45g)	plain (semi-sweet) chocolate	1¹/₂ oz
1 tbs	cornflour (cornstarch)	1 tbs
4 tbs	water	4 tbs

1   Put the flour and salt in a bowl, blend in the margarine and add enough water to make a dough. Roll it out, put it into a flan dish, prick with a fork, and bake in the oven at 425°F (220°C, Gas Mark 7) for 10 minutes. Remove from the oven.
2   Put the tofu, all the sugar except 1 tbs, 1 tsp of the vanilla essence, and the oil in a liquidizer and blend thoroughly. Pour into the partially baked pie shell, return to the oven and bake at 350°F (180°C, Gas Mark 4) for half an hour.
3   Melt the chocolate in a basin or small saucepan over a saucepan of boiling water. Stir in the remaining sugar and vanilla essence. Dissolve the cornflour (cornstarch) in the water and stir into the chocolate. Continue stirring until the mixture has thickened.
4   Spoon the chocolate mixture over the baked pie. Leave to cool, then chill until ready to serve.

Coconut custard pie

IMPERIAL/METRIC		AMERICAN
6 oz (170g)	vegetarian digestive biscuits (graham crackers)	6 oz
2 oz (55g)	vegetable margarine	$^1/_4$ cup
$^3/_4$ lb (340g)	medium tofu	$1^1/_2$ cups
4 tbs	vegetable oil	4 tbs
1 tsp	vanilla essence	1 tsp
$^1/_4$ tsp	sea salt	$^1/_4$ tsp
3–4 oz (85–115g)	raw cane sugar	$^1/_2$–$^3/_4$ cup
$3^1/_2$ oz (100g)	desiccated (shredded) coconut	$1^1/_4$ cups

1 Grind the biscuits (graham crackers) finely (or crush with a rolling pin). Melt the margarine and mix with the crumbs. Turn into a greased flan tin and pat down firmly. Bake in the oven at 375°F (190°C, Gas Mark 5) for 15 minutes then remove from the oven.
2 Put the tofu, oil, vanilla essence, salt and sugar into a liquidizer and blend thoroughly. Stir in 3 oz (85g, 1 cup) of the coconut.
3 Pour the mixture into the crumb shell and bake at 350°F (180°C, Gas Mark 4) for 15 minutes. Sprinkle the top with the remaining coconut and bake for about 5 minutes longer. Remove from the oven, cool, then chill before serving.

Honeyed tofu and yogurt pie

IMPERIAL/METRIC		AMERICAN
¹/₂–³/₄ lb (225–340g)	firm tofu	1–1¹/₂ cups
¹/₂ pint (285ml)	soya (soy) yogurt	1¹/₃ cups
4 tbs	honey	4 tbs
1 tsp	vanilla essence	1 tsp
1	pre-baked wholewheat pastry shell	1
as required	fresh fruit (e.g. strawberries, bananas, peaches, kiwi fruit)	as required

1 Put the tofu into a clean tea towel (dish towel) and squeeze until the liquid has been extracted. Put into a mixing bowl and add the yogurt, honey and vanilla essence. Beat well.
2 Spoon the tofu mixture into the baked pie shell, cover and chill for several hours.
3 When ready to serve top with sliced fresh fruit.

Avocado and tofu dessert

This is similar in kind to the four preceding recipes. It is nice and simple but also rich and satisfying.

IMPERIAL/METRIC		AMERICAN
4 oz (115g)	vegetarian digestive biscuits (graham crackers)	4 oz
3 tbs	vegetable margarine	3 tbs
2 small or 1 large	ripe avocado	2 small or 1 large
³/₄ lb (340g)	firm tofu	1¹/₂ cups
2 tbs	soya (soy) yogurt	2 tbs
2 oz (55g)	raw cane sugar	4 tbs
juice and rind of ¹/₂	lemon	juice and rind of ¹/₂

1 Crush the biscuits (graham crackers). Melt the margarine and mix in the crumbs. Divide between 4 individual serving dishes and press down well. Chill.
2 Peel the avocado and chop coarsely. Put the avocado, tofu, yogurt, sugar, lemon juice and rind into a liquidizer and blend thoroughly.
3 Pour the avocado mixture on top of the crumb bases. Chill before serving.

Here are three recipes for the simplest desserts imaginable.

Apricot cream

IMPERIAL/METRIC		AMERICAN
4–6 oz (115–170g)	dried apricots	1 cup
$^1/_2$–$^3/_4$ lb (225–340g)	medium or firm tofu	1–1$^1/_2$ cups
2–3 tsp	lemon juice	2–3 tsp
2 oz (55g)	raw cane sugar	4 tbs
2 tbs	soya (soy) yogurt	2 tbs
3–4 tbs	flaked (slivered) almonds	3–4 tbs

1 Soak the apricots in water for several hours or steam until tender (apricots that have been cooked will give a creamier texture; apricots that have simply been soaked will have a chewier texture).
2 Combine all the ingredients except the almonds in a liquidizer and blend thoroughly.
3 Pour into dessert dishes and top with the almonds. Serve chilled.

Strawberry cream

IMPERIAL/METRIC		AMERICAN
1 lb (455g)	fresh strawberries	1 lb
$^3/_4$ lb (340g)	medium or firm tofu	1$^1/_2$ cups
juice of 1	lemon	juice of 1
2–3 oz (55–85g)	raw cane sugar	4–6 tbs
$^1/_4$ tsp	vanilla essence	$^1/_4$ tsp

1 Leave aside a few of the nicest strawberries. Put all the rest in a liquidizer with the other ingredients and blend thoroughly.
2 Pour into dessert dishes and decorate with the strawberries that have been set aside. Serve chilled.

Pineapple cream

This recipe contains honey, though you could substitute sugar to taste.

IMPERIAL/METRIC		AMERICAN
1 tin (about 14 oz [400g])	pineapple in its own juice	1 can (14–16 oz)
$^3/_4$ lb (340g)	medium tofu	$1^1/_2$ cups
2 oz (55g)	honey	$^1/_6$ cup
1 tbs	vegetable oil	1 tbs

1   Put the pineapple into a liquidizer with the tofu, honey, oil, and about 1 tbs juice from the tin. Blend thoroughly.
2   Pour into dessert dishes and chill well before serving.

Sweet tofu fritters

An exotic dessert which is not difficult to make. Orange flower water is available at specialist delicatessens and food halls.

IMPERIAL/METRIC		AMERICAN
$^1/_2$ lb (225g)	firm tofu	1 cup
2 oz (55g)	wholewheat flour	$^1/_2$ cup
1 tbs	honey	1 tbs
2 tsp	orange flower water	2 tsp
as required	vegetable oil for deep-frying	as required
$^1/_2$ lb (225g)	apricot jam	$^1/_2$ lb
4 tbs	water	4 tbs

1   Mash the tofu in a mixing bowl. Stir in the flour, honey, and 1 tsp of the orange flower water.
2   Form the tofu mixture into walnut-sized mounds and deep-fry in the oil until golden brown. Drain and keep warm.

3   Heat the apricot jam in a small saucepan. Add the water and the remaining orange flower water. Bring to the boil.
4   Serve the fritters warm with the hot apricot sauce poured over them.

Tofu is used as an ingredient in most American non-dairy ice-creams and some British ones as well. The problem with making any kind of ice-cream at home is that it requires churning, a laborious process by hand. Compact, easy-to-use ice-cream makers are now readily available, and I strongly recommend them for these recipes. The first is a basic recipe which can be flavoured in many other ways.

Vanilla ice-cream

IMPERIAL/METRIC		AMERICAN
¹/₂ lb (225g)	soft or medium tofu	1 cup
2 tsp	vanilla essence	2 tsp
2 tbs	vegetable oil	2 tbs
2–3 oz (55–85g)	raw cane sugar	4–6 tbs
¹/₃ pint (200ml)	soya (soy) milk	³/₄ cup

1   Combine all the ingredients in a liquidizer and blend thoroughly.
2   For best results use an ice-cream maker. Otherwise, pour the mixture into a suitable container and put in a freezer. Stir frequently while it is freezing to avoid crystallization. Transfer the ice-cream from the freezer to the refrigerator 10–15 minutes before serving.

Maple walnut tofu ice-cream

IMPERIAL/METRIC		AMERICAN
2 oz (55g)	soft or medium tofu	$^1/_4$ cup
$^1/_4$ pint (140ml)	soya (soy) milk	$^2/_3$ cup
1 oz (30g)	soft vegetarian margarine	2 tbs
$^1/_4$ pint (140ml)	maple essence	$^2/_3$ cup
1 tsp	vanilla syrup	1 tsp
pinch	sea salt	pinch
2 oz (55g)	walnut pieces	$^1/_2$ cup

1 Put all the ingredients except the walnut pieces into a liquidizer and blend thoroughly.
2 Stir in the walnut pieces (if they are large ones then break or chop them into small pieces).
3 Freeze in an ice-cream maker, or in a freezer following the instructions for Vanilla ice-cream.

Raspberry tofu ice-cream

IMPERIAL/METRIC		AMERICAN
$^1/_2$ lb (225g)	soft or medium tofu	1 cup
4 tbs	soya (soy) milk	4 tbs
2 oz (55g)	raw cane sugar	4 tbs
2 tbs	vegetable oil	2 tbs
pinch	sea salt	pinch
$^1/_2$ lb (225g)	fresh or defrosted frozen raspberries	$^1/_2$ lb
1 tsp	lemon juice	1 tsp
$^1/_2$ tsp	vanilla essence	$^1/_2$ tsp
2–3 drops	almond essence	2–3 drops

1 Put the tofu, milk, sugar, oil and salt in a liquidizer and blend thoroughly.
2 Sieve the raspberries, discard the seeds, and add this purée to the liquidizer along with the lemon juice, vanilla and almond essences. Blend thoroughly.
3 Freeze in an ice-cream maker, or in a freezer following the instructions for Vanilla ice-cream.

Fruit fools are traditionally made with cream and/or custard. Below are two recipes which require neither.

Gooseberry fool

IMPERIAL/METRIC		AMERICAN
³/₄ lb (340g)	gooseberries	³/₄ lb
4–5 tbs (or to taste)	raw cane sugar	4–5 tbs (or to taste)
³/₄ lb (340g)	medium tofu	1¹/₂ cups
pinch	sea salt	pinch
¹/₂ tsp	lemon juice	¹/₂ tsp
2 tbs	vegetable oil	2 tbs
4–5 tbs	water	4–5 tbs

1 Wash, top and tail gooseberries. Put them in a saucepan with the water and sugar, bring to the boil, then lower the heat and simmer until tender. Leave to cool.
2 Put the tofu, salt, lemon juice and oil in a liquidizer, then add the cooked gooseberries. Blend the mixture thoroughly, stirring it between blending, until well mixed.
3 Transfer to dessert dishes and serve chilled.

Rhubarb fool

IMPERIAL/METRIC		AMERICAN
1 lb (455g)	rhubarb	1 lb
6 tbs	water	6 tbs
6 oz (170g)	raw cane sugar	1 cup
$^{1}/_{2}$ tsp	powdered agar-agar	$^{1}/_{2}$ tsp
$^{3}/_{4}$ lb (340g)	medium tofu	1$^{1}/_{2}$ cups
pinch	sea salt	pinch
$^{1}/_{2}$ tsp	lemon juice	$^{1}/_{2}$ tsp
2 tbs	vegetable oil	2 tbs

1   Chop the rhubarb into small pieces. Place in a saucepan with the water and about two-thirds of the sugar. Bring to the boil, then lower the heat, cover and simmer until the fruit is well cooked. Sprinkle in the agar-agar, raise the heat a little and stir. Leave to simmer for a minute longer. Remove from the heat and leave to cool briefly.
2   Put the tofu, salt, lemon juice, oil and remaining sugar in a liquidizer, then add the rhubarb. Blend very thoroughly.
3   Pour into serving dishes and chill.

Tofu strudel

This would make a pleasant dinner-party dessert.

IMPERIAL/METRIC		AMERICAN
³/₄ lb (340g)	firm or medium tofu	1¹/₂ cups
2 tbs	soya (soy) yogurt	2 tbs
2 oz (55g)	raisins	¹/₃ cup
1 tsp	vanilla essence	1 tsp
3 oz (85g)	raw cane sugar	¹/₂ cup
2 tbs	vegetable margarine	2 tbs
8 sheets	frozen filo pastry, thawed	8 sheets
as required	sieved icing (powdered) sugar or finely ground raw cane sugar	as required

1   Put the tofu into a clean tea towel (dish towel) and squeeze well to extract as much moisture as possible. Put the tofu into a mixing bowl and add the yogurt, raisins, vanilla essence and sugar. Mix thoroughly.
2   Melt the margarine. Spread a little melted margarine on each sheet of pastry, then spread one-eighth of the tofu mixture over. Roll up the sheet and turn the ends over. Place on an oiled baking sheet.
3   When all 8 sheets have been filled, bake in the oven at 425°F (220°C, Gas Mark 7) for 20–30 minutes, until lightly browned.
4   Sprinkle with icing (powdered) sugar or finely ground raw cane sugar and serve warm if possible.

Hungarian-style layered pancakes

This is undoubtedly the most time-consuming recipe in this chapter, but for anyone with a strongly developed sweet tooth the results cannot fail to impress.

IMPERIAL/METRIC		AMERICAN
	Batter:	
5 oz (140g)	wholewheat flour	1¼ cups
2 tbs	soya (soy) flour	2 tbs
1 tsp	baking powder	1 tsp
pinch	sea salt	pinch
2 tsp plus additional for frying	vegetable oil	2 tsp plus additional for frying
4 oz (115g)	firm or medium tofu	½ cup
2 tsp	raw cane sugar	2 tsp
1 tbs	soya (soy) yogurt	1 tbs
2 tsp	lemon juice	2 tsp
grated rind of ½	lemon	grated rind of ½
3–4 tbs	apricot jam	3–4 tbs
2 oz (55g)	hazelnuts, almonds or walnuts	½ cup
2 oz (55g)	plain (semi-sweet) chocolate	2 oz
1 oz (30g)	creamed coconut	2 tbs
1 tbs	hot water	1 tbs
	bottled chocolate sauce (optional)	

1 To make the batter, mix the flour, soya (soy) flour, baking powder and salt together in a bowl. Add the 2 tsp oil, then add a little water at a time, mixing in with a fork until the mixture is the consistency of thick cream. Leave it to stand for half an hour or more. (If it is then too thick add a little more water; if too thin a little more flour.)

2 Mash the tofu in a bowl. Stir in the sugar, yogurt, lemon juice and lemon rind.

3 Heat the jam slightly.

4　Grind the nuts finely. Grate the chocolate. Mix the ground nuts and chocolate together.

5　Fry the pancakes on both sides in a little oil. Place the first pancake on an oiled pie dish. Spread a layer of the tofu mixture on top. Fry the next pancake; put it on top of the tofu mixture then spread with a layer of apricot jam. Fry a third pancake, put it on top, and spread some of the nut and chocolate mixture on top. Continue layering until all the ingredients have been used, finishing up with a pancake on top.

6　Grate or finely chop the creamed coconut and mix with the hot water. Spread over the top pancake. Bake in the oven at 375°F (190°C, Gas Mark 5) for 15–20 minutes.

7　Remove from the oven and slice into 4 wedges. Serve hot, with a bottled chocolate sauce poured over the top if desired.

Quick and easy recipes, recipes suitable for a single portion, and recipes suitable for a dinner party

Index